Praise for *Vector Basic Training*

"The problem with vector images today is that I hate most of them! Mainly because something dies between the drawing and the precision vector graphic version. Perhaps it's the illustration's soul lost in the transition? Most vector images today contain too many cyber-slick gradations, they are too mathematically perfect, like many of the billions of images populating millions of microstock sites that lack anything real and human. If Von's book can help improve a designer's ability to create better vector images, I'm all for it. And remember: Just because you can make everything a gradation doesn't mean you should make everything a gradation."

— **CHARLES ANDERSON**, CSA Design

"With *Vector Basic Training*, Von Glitschka shames me. And I thank him for it. He reminds me that I am walking a tightrope of forsaking my first love: drawing. Von approaches the process with an honor and reverence that emerges from a tradition rooted in art as much as design. His depth of thought, trained hand, and ability to art direct himself has produced a stunning body of work and he brings it all home in *VBT* to share with the reader. That's the thing with Von—not only is he a powerful talent, he's gracious enough to share it all. I'll be keeping my copy of *VBT* next to my Mac and, yes, my sketchpad."

— **TERRY MARKS**, TMARKS Design

"Von's experience as an award-winning 'illustrative designer' enables him to provide a valuable methodology for creating vector artwork guaranteed to produce results for every designer."

— **EARL GEE**, Creative Director, Gee + Chung Design

"As president of the School of Advertising Art (saa), I would like to thank Von for writing this book. Young designers need to understand the power of the drawing process, and they need to know that time spent sketching before jumping to the computer is time well spent on any project. Von clearly demonstrates this philosophy throughout the book by incorporating interesting visual examples of his work. I am excited to share *Vector Basic Training* with SAA students."

— **JESSICA GRAVES**, President, School of Advertising Art, Kettering, Ohio

FROM THE DEPARTMENT OF ILLUSTRATIVE DESIGN

Vector
BASIC TRAINING

A SYSTEMATIC CREATIVE PROCESS
FOR BUILDING PRECISION VECTOR ARTWORK

DEVELOPED & WRITTEN BY
VON GLITSCHKA

VECTOR BASIC TRAINING:
A Systematic Creative Process for Building Precision Vector Artwork

Von Glitschka

New Riders
1249 Eighth Street
Berkeley, CA 94710
510/524-2178
510/524-2221 (fax)

Find us on the Web at: www.newriders.com
To report errors, please send a note to errata@peachpit.com
New Riders is an imprint of Peachpit, a division of Pearson Education.

Project Editor: Nikki Echler McDonald
Development Editor: Cathy Fishel-Lane
Production Editor: Tracey Croom
Proofreader: Liz Welch
Indexer: Ken Della Penta
Cover Design: Von Glitschka
Composition and Interior Design: Kim Scott, Bumpy Design
Media Producer: Eric Geoffroy
Video Producer: Mary Sweeney

ISBN 13: 978-0-321-74959-8
ISBN 10:   0-321-74959-6

9 8 7 6 5 4 3 2 1

Printed and bound in the United States of America

To my two wonderful daughters, Savannah and Alyssa.
You both inspire me in such unique and funny ways at times.
I love when you two make me laugh, and seeing you both
exercise your creativity is a joy to my heart. I love you both so
very much, and I look forward to seeing you both grow up into
beautiful young women.

— Pa

Acknowledgements

The first and foremost person I need to thank is my lovely wife Rebecca. Her understanding and support for my work over the years is a living demonstration of caring patience and wisdom. I've spent many months writing this book and numerous late-night creative sessions compiling its content, and she graciously supported me every step of the way. Love you, Becky!

When I was first approached by Peachpit acquisitions editor Nikki "The Whip" McDonald to write a book, I wasn't sure if the project was a good fit for me, or for Peachpit. After wrestling with the idea, I initially turned it down. But Nikki, being a relentless and gentle persuader, encouraged me to reconsider. She also listened to my concerns and provided both answers and a shared vision. I couldn't be happier with the end result. Thanks, Nikki.

There is only one person who has shown me more about English than Cathy "Soothsayer" Fishel-Lane, and that would be my high school English teacher Mr. Parsons. Unfortunately, I spent most of my time drawing in his class. So I'm very thankful to have a rockstar editor like Cathy performing textual plastic surgery on my bad grammar and improper use of industry nomenclature. Thanks for making me read smarter than I sound in real life, Cathy.

When it comes to the technical aspects of video production, I'm about as informed as a small neck clam. The guidance and coaching I received from Mary "Zapruder" Sweeney made the work as painless as possible, so thank you for your dedication and help. I appreciate it.

A big techno thank you also goes to colleague Jean-Claude "Van Damme" Tremblay, whose expert tech-editing and suggestions improved the accuracy of what you'll be reading. Thanks, Jean-Claude.

To everyone else on the Peachpit team, including design manager Charlene Will, production editor Tracey Croom, and designer Kim Scott: You have a well-thought-out process that made working with you not only easy, but precise. My OCD tendencies thank you. And knowing that Peachpit prints the vast majority of its books, including this one, here in the United States, is just icing on the publishing cake.

To my fellow design friends with whom I shared as I created this book (you know who you are): Thank you for your willing feedback and suggestions at critical times. It helped me break through mental walls and keep moving forward on this project.

To all of you who follow me on Twitter, Facebook, or who subscribe to my blog: You've read my numerous laments and rants over the years about all manner of industry-related issues. Thank you for understanding, agreeing, sharing in return, laughing with me, laughing at me, unfollowing me, RT'ing me, forwarding my link to your friends, or posting snarky retorts telling me to chill out. This book is for you. So stop reading this stuff and dive into the content already. Sheesh.

About the Author

Von Glitschka is principal of Glitschka Studios and has worked in the communication arts industry for over 23 years. His work reflects the symbiotic relationship between design and illustration. This duality of skills within his own creative arsenal inspired him to coin the phrase and title "Illustrative Designer."

Photo by Tim Adams

In 2002, Glitschka founded Glitschka Studios, a multi-disciplinary creative firm. The studio shines as a hired gun for ad agencies, medium-to-large design firms, and in-house corporate art departments working on a diverse range of illustrative design projects.

His exuberant graphics have garnered numerous design and illustration awards and have appeared in such publications as *Communication Arts*, *Print*, *HOW*, Society of Illustrators annuals, *Graphis*, *American Illustration* books, and *LogoLounge II*, *III*, *IV*, *V*, and *VI*.

Glitschka has spoken nationally at the HOW Design Conference, Adobe MAX Conference, The Illustration Conference (ICON), AIGA chapter events, ADFED groups, design schools, in-house art departments, and marketing groups.

His mix of humor, inspiration, great design, and solid creative methodology are all part of his presentation productions, which always draw a large following.

Glitschka works out of his home studio in the Pacific Northwest (Land of Bigfoot) and can usually be found spending an unhealthy amount of time on Twitter conversing in all manner of witty banter and sarcasm. Follow him at @vonster or visit his website at www.vonglitschka.com.

CONTENTS

INTRODUCTION xi

CHAPTER 1 **BÉZIER CURVES: A BRIEF HISTORY** 1

Fear of Math 2

Who Created Bézier Curves? 3

What Is a Bézier Curve? 6

DESIGN DRILLS: Behind the Vector Curtain 11

CHAPTER 2 **YOUR CREATIVE ARMAMENT** 15

A Love-Hate Relationship 16

Core Tools for Vector Building 17

Customize Your Environment 26

Stop Re-creating the Wheel 29

DESIGN DRILLS: Deconstructing Design 35

CHAPTER 3 **ANALOG METHODS IN A DIGITAL AGE** 41

Don't Be a Tooler 42

I Get Paid to Draw 43

Concepts and Ideas 44

Analog Tools 45

The Lost Art of Thumbnailing 45

Refine Your Drawing 49

Systematic and Creative 57

DESIGN DRILLS: Essential Nonsense 63

CHAPTER 4 **GETTING TO THE POINTS** **71**

The Good Anchor Point and Path 72

The Bad Anchor Point and Path 74

The Ugly Anchor Point and Path 75

A Scrutinizing Eye 76

A Good Example 80

DESIGN DRILLS: Vector Skeletons 83

CHAPTER 5 **SHAPE SURVEILLANCE** **87**

The Clockwork Method 88

Prime Point Placement 100

Deconstructing the Vector Monster 108

Progressive Improvements 112

DESIGN DRILLS: Spotting Clocks 113

CHAPTER 6 **VECTOR BUILD METHODS** **117**

Point-by-Point Method 120

Shape-Building Method 126

BetterHandles Plug-in 134

E Pluribus Buildum 136

Symmetry Is Your Friend 139

A Healthy Creative Process 145

DESIGN DRILLS: Fast and Easy 147

CHAPTER 7 **STYLE APPROPRIATE** **151**

Design Chameleons 152

DESIGN DRILLS: Use It or Lose It 175

CHAPTER 8 **ART DIRECTING YOURSELF** 181

Fresh Eyes Effect 182

Your Inner Art Director 185

Avoid Visual Tension 189

Full-Tilt Creative Boogie 194

DESIGN DRILLS: Hop to It 195

CHAPTER 9 **GOOD CREATIVE HABITS** 201

Doodle Binders 203

Layers Are Your Friend 205

Colors and File Naming 219

Last, But Not Least 221

DESIGN DRILLS: Top-Eight List 223

INDEX 231

Introduction

Vector Basic Training

The one question I get asked most by other creatives is, "How do you get your vector artwork to look so nice?" When people ask me this, they're not talking about any specific art project or illustration, but rather how I go about building my artwork in vector format so precisely.

Truth is that many designers, whether they are students or seasoned professionals, struggle with building precise vector shapes. I have wrestled with it myself. There are times I have to access old art files from my personal archive, and when I open them, I cringe, thinking, "Why did I build it that way?" or "That could have been done a lot better."

The point is: We all have room for improvement.

Vector Basic Training exhaustively documents my own creative process and approach to building vector artwork. The methods I'll cover in this book (with exception to the plug-ins covered in chapter 2) are what I'd call application-agnostic. No specific software is required because you'll be able to take these methods and use them within the vector drawing application of your choice. For sake of demonstration, I'll be using Adobe Illustrator, which is the drawing application of *my* choice.

This book isn't your typical software-oriented technical manual or a how-to for using the latest tools and pull-down menu effects. It assumes you have a general understanding of vector drawing applications already and want to improve your skills so you can build precise vector artwork.

My creative process is systematic in its approach. You may not agree with everything I have to say, but you can't argue with the end results you'll be able to produce over time if you apply the methods to your own creative endeavors.

Why Designers Should Draw

Yes, this is a book about vector build methods, but its creative foundation is firmly established on core drawing skills—something I stress repeatedly throughout this book because I feel so strongly about its importance to the creative process.

We all drew pictures when we were children, freely and joyfully with arms and legs protruding madly from the heads of our very first crudely rendered self-portraits. Many of you continued to draw as you grew older and that creative passion is probably one of the main reasons you're a designer today.

Some of you, however, didn't stick with drawing and have evolved into the type of designer who can't, or simply doesn't, draw. This is unacceptable.

If you drew every day, in five years you certainly would not say to yourself, "I wish I never would have started drawing again. I am a worse designer now." Your creative skills will only improve by integrating drawing into your creative process. The practical benefits from drawing will be self-evident and a lot of fun.

I should point out that when I say "drawing" I don't mean that everyone needs to become a full-fledged illustrator. Being able to draw allows you to take the ethereal concept in your mind and formulate it visually. The more you draw, the better you're able to capture and leverage ideas and expand your creative potential. Combine improved drawing skills with the vector build methods in this book, and you will definitely execute better artwork with more precision.

When it's all said and done, you'll be what I like to call a "drawsigner."

Digital vs. Analog

Even though our industry may be digitally driven, ideas are still best developed in analog form. You should always work out your ideas by drawing out your visual explorations on paper before you ever jump onto a computer. Failure to do so is the primary cause of many designers' problems when building vector artwork. If you can't draw accurately on paper, you won't be able to draw accurately on a computer either.

Building vector artwork before you know exactly what to build is an exercise in design futility. In this book, I'll show you how to utilize both analog and digital methods throughout the entire creative process. You'll learn how to go back and forth between the two realms to create effective and precise vector artwork.

As part of the creative process that I'll teach you in this book, I'll ask you to start by drawing out your ideas as thumbnail sketches using good old-fashioned pencil, pen, and paper. After refining your sketchwork, we'll scan it into a drawing application and begin our vector build process. I have several tried-and-true methods and build processes, which I'll explain throughout this book, that will give you a firm understanding of how to place just the right amount of points in just the right places for any design. The end result? Precision vector graphics nearly every time.

Process Makes Perfect

You've heard the saying, "Practice makes perfect." But I'd argue that when building vector art, your process must be precise from the start. A flawed or sloppy creative process will handicap your design potential. Worse, repeated over time, it will make you a consistent builder of marginal vector artwork.

I think a more accurate saying for our purposes would be, "Process makes perfect." This book will help you establish a successful creative process that you can use on any project type and that, over time, will improve your creative abilities so that you can design well-crafted artwork consistently.

Direct to DVD

The build methods and plug-ins showcased in this book are also thoroughly documented in action through more than four hours of screencasts, which are included on the DVD. You'll also find helpful resource files so you can test drive these methods yourself and deconstruct art shown in the book so that you can better understand how it was built.

When you see the DVD camera icon anywhere in the book, it means the content provided on that page has a video on the DVD that is associated with it.

When you see the Resource Ai icon appear in the book, it means the content being discussed on that page has a vector source file associated with it that is provided on the DVD. Again, these are yours to play with and study.

Don't be a Design-O-Saur

Nothing hangs me up more in my workflow than an unforeseen software bug or computer problem. I've often thought what it would be like if other industries had to deal with the types of problems we face all the time.

Imagine, for example, if a construction worker backed his truck over his tool belt and broke his hammer in half, forcing him to head to the local hardware store and buy a new hammer. The man returns to the work site to finish the job, but when tries to use the new hammer to drive in some nails, the hammer shifts to the right, causing the construction worker to hit the board instead of the nail. Uh-oh—looks like his new hammer isn't compatible with his older version nails.

I know this is silly, but it's the type of reality we designers have to deal with every day.

Our industry, more than most, is in constant flux due to the ever-growing and changing technologies we have to work with on a daily basis. It can get overwhelming at times keeping up to speed with everything, but it's essential in order to stay creatively relevant with the larger design community.

A creative process should be flexible enough to accommodate new technology, methods, and tools that will improve its efficiency without compromising its effectiveness.

Vector Basic Training won't cover every possible tool for building vector art, but it will introduce you to a systematic creative process that you can use to create high-quality design work, regardless of which vector drawing program you use.

Along the way, I'll touch on additional tools and techniques that make certain vector build methods easier to accomplish. The methodology I cover may stretch your creative comfort zone, but unless you adapt to new methods and constantly strive to improve your design skills, you risk becoming a dreaded *design-o-saur*, and your once forward-looking design work will start to resemble a thing of the past.

FIELD NOTES

A Systematic Creative Process

Having a plan of creative attack as you approach any given design project is essential in order to produce work that is both appropriate and effective for your clients. Here is how my creative process breaks down into specific stages:

1. Research
2. Style Selection
3. Thumbnail Sketching
4. Refinement Sketches
5. Building Your Artwork
6. Final Artwork

Vector Basic Training will serve as your field guide to creative excellence, covering all these topics and more, so you'll be better equipped to approach your own work and grow your skills moving forward.

CHAPTER 1

Bézier Curves: A Brief History

My first year at Lydia Hawk Elementary School was the last year first-grade teacher Mrs. Jenkins would teach before retiring. In hindsight, I can see she was a mean-spirited, elderly lady way past due for retirement. She also bore a striking resemblance to "The Church Lady" from the famous *Saturday Night Live* skit. At the time, of course, I didn't think that. I just thought this was what school was all about.

Fear of Math

I remember the day like it was yesterday. Mrs. Jerkins had called me up to the chalkboard to solve a math problem. As was her practice, she stood scowling off to the side of the chalkboard as I approached. In one hand, she held a rubber-tipped wooden dowel, and in the other, she gripped a chain that hung from an intercom speaker with which she could call the office in one quick, furious pull.

For what seemed like an eternity, I stood with my face a few inches from the chalkboard, staring at the math problem with no clue of how to solve it. Nervously, I turned to Mrs. Jerkins and asked, "How do I do it?"

In response, she furrowed her brow and angrily slapped the wooden dowel against the chalkboard, saying, "Solve the problem or I call the office!"

I knew I couldn't give her the correct answer. Frustrated, I began to cry. From that point forward, I loathed math. It scared me.

FIGURE 1.1 I suppose Pythagoras might have tied a harelip on Mrs. Jerkins for giving math such a bum rap in my mind.

Math Is Cool

Throughout the remainder of my school years, I both feared and loathed math. When I started thinking about college, I chose art school because I loved art and was excited by the possibility of drawing for a living. But, to be honest, I also thought to myself, "Plus, art school won't have any math classes!"

But, as some kids learn to appreciate things like Brussels sprouts, sushi, and a well-aged cheese plate as they grow older, I've learned to appreciate math. Over the years, I've come to realize just how much math is a part of everything we experience in life. And, the more I've learned about building vector shapes with Bézier curves, the more I've come to appreciate the geometric equations that compose my art.

Even though I'm not that great at math myself—my daughter's fourth-grade homework has been known to stump me—math no longer scares the bejeezus out of me. In fact, I think it's pretty cool. And it's behind all of the digital art we create.

Who Created Bézier Curves?

I won't pretend to be an expert in math history, but I've done enough sleuthing to trace the family history of the modern Bézier curve, which forms the basis of all vector drawing programs in use today. An understanding of this history won't improve your drawing skills, but it will give you a better appreciation of the tools we use.

The Vector Family Tree

Mathematics is an ever-expanding knowledge base driven by fertile minds. One person's work in the field has historically enabled the next generation to progress and evolve. The vector family tree that fruited the Bézier curve sprouted from this same form of progressive development, by way of four key individuals:

1. **Karl Weierstrass** (1815–1897): A German mathematician who created the Weierstrass theorem, which stated (in very basic terms here) that any function or set of data points can be modeled with a polynomial. A polynomial is an algebraic equation that sounds scary, but is actually the vector artist's best buddy. Suffice it to say that simple polynomials are very easy to graph, as they produce smooth and continuous curves or lines. Sound familiar?

2. **Sergei Natanovich Bernstein** (1880–1968): A Jewish Soviet mathematician who proved the Weierstrass theorem through his own namesake, Bernstein polynomials.

3. **Paul de Casteljau** (1930–1999): The French physicist and mathematician who worked for the car maker, Citroën. De Casteljau used Bernstein's polynomials to invent the de Casteljau algorithm (just a step-by-step solution to figure out a problem) for computing Bézier curves, which enabled Citroën to accurately create more beautiful curves in its vehicles (FIGURE 1.2).

4. **Pierre Bézier** (1910–1999): The French contemporary of Paul de Casteljau, Bézier was an engineer who worked for the car manufacturer Renault. He is directly responsible for patenting and popularizing Bézier curves within a digital context through the development of CAD/CAM software, and because of that, Bézier curves bear his name (FIGURE 1.3).

Before Bézier curves, it was impossible to create graceful or elegant curves on early CAD/CAM systems. As the technology developed in the 1970s and 1980s, it appeared in Illustrator and then in FreeHand.

Personally, I think de Casteljau got shafted on the legacy end of things. After all, he was the rightful inventor. But, then again, "de Casteljau curves" just doesn't roll off the tongue half as easy as "Bézier curves."

Bézier curves might be math-driven, but it was the design thinkers who breathed life into those equations and used them to form something beautiful.

As much as I think analog methods, such as drawing, are vital to the creative process, I can't imagine doing my job without my digital tools. I'm a geek: I love my Mac, and I thoroughly enjoy how it equips my creativity and makes my work flow so easily.

We can all thank Pierre Bézier for taking Bézier curves from analog to digital, making Bézier curves as ubiquitous in the design industry as black clothes and designer frames.

FIGURE 1.2 Paul de Casteljau used Bézier curves to aid in creating well-rounded car designs for Citroën.

FIGURE 1.3 My illustration of Pierre Bézier, a.k.a. "The French Curve."

What Is a Bézier Curve?

So what does the mathematical equation of a Bézier curve look like? I asked Bill Casselman, professor of mathematics at the University of British Columbia, to give us a peek at a basic Bézier curve and the math behind the art (FIGURE 1.4).

FIGURE 1.4 A basic Bézier curve and its mathematical equation, created by Dr. Bill Casselman.

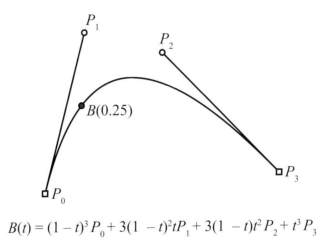

$$B(t) = (1-t)^3 P_0 + 3(1-t)^2 t P_1 + 3(1-t)t^2 P_2 + t^3 P_3$$

I think it's safe to say you'd have an easier time learning to speak Klingon than trying to wrap your brain around the math required to create a Bézier curve. And thanks to Pierre Bézier, you'll never have to. All you really need to know is that vector art is made up of anchor points and paths and that a Bézier curve is any segment of that path between two anchor points that requires a curved shape. One piece of art can have thousands of Bézier curves in it, as shown in FIGURE 1.5.

Put even more simply, a Bézier curve is a path that you can bend from one end or the other using the handle bars extended from the anchor points at each end of the path.

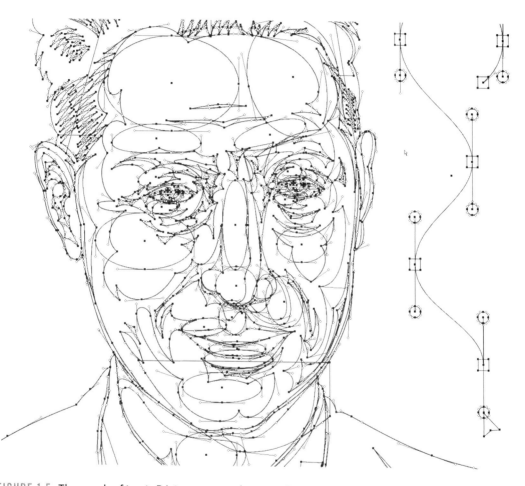

FIGURE 1.5 Thousands of ironic Bézier curves make up my Pierre Bézier illustration.

When to Use a Bézier Curve

Odds are good that if your vector drawing has curves in it, you'll be using Bézier curves to build it. A Bézier curve will have handlebars that protrude out of the various anchor points in your design. You use these to control and manipulate the curves so you can create the exact shapes you need for your design. The more organic and free-form your design is, the more likely you'll need to manipulate Bézier curves to build the vector shapes. It's impossible to get elegant and graceful curves without them (**FIGURE 1.6**).

That said, you won't need to use Bézier curves for every project. For example, if you're creating an image that's chunky and graphic—without smooth curves—you can use just anchor points and paths. I didn't need to grab the handle bars at all when creating **FIGURE 1.7** (that said, see the Field Notes at the end of this chapter).

Knowing when to use a Bézier curve and when not to has a lot to do with what you're creating. In Chapter 6, "Rules of Creative Engagement," we'll go into more detail about vector build methods and discuss how they can help *or* hinder your final art.

FIGURE 1.6 This funky "C" uses nothing but Bézier curves and handles.

FIGURE 1.7 This chunky, graphic "C" uses no Bézier curves, thus no handlebars were needed.

A Beautiful Irony

The use of Bézier curves in vector-based graphic programs has transformed our industry. We can now take our pen and paper ideas and build them precisely using digital tools. This method allows us to scale our work to any size without degrading its quality and makes repurposing our work easier than ever before.

It was math that created the Bézier curve, but it was artists (many of whom were likely math-phobic) who took those curves and who can now use them to tell fantastic visual stories.

It's a beautiful irony, and for that I say, "Viva Bézier!"

FIELD NOTES

Vector Detailing Trick

When you create artwork that is chunky, like the "C" shown in Figure 1.7, you *can* build it using just points and paths, but I recommend building it with Bézier curves. You can use Bézier curves to create very subtle curves between the anchor points so that the line isn't absolutely straight.

This is a method I use to improve the visual aesthetics of my design work. Simply using the computer to create art runs the risk of creating work that is too perfect, too straight, too sterile.

Infusing my design with these delicate Bézier curves makes it more natural in its final form and makes it feel less computerized.

DESIGN DRILLS:
Behind the Vector Curtain

Whenever you're working in Adobe Illustrator, you can toggle between Preview and Outline mode (Command-Y or Control-Y) to see the raw vector work behind your design. Flipping to outline mode is a fast and easy way to see how Bézier curves make vector art possible.

In fact, the earliest version of Illustrator forced you to build all of your art in Outline mode. You could only take sneak peeks using Preview to visually gauge your progress. But then you'd have to revert back to Outline mode to continue building or editing your vectors.

This all changed when another drawing program, Aldus FreeHand, was released. It allowed its users to build in Preview mode, which made the whole process far easier and more intuitive. Eventually, Illustrator adapted the same modus operandi.

Let's take a sneak peek behind the vector curtain and view the Bézier curves of three designs from my project archives. I've selected these because they represent three distinctly different styles and project types. Styles and project types vary, but the fundamental Bézier curve structure behind them all works the same. A simple style such as shown in FIGURE 1.12 takes far fewer Bézier curves to pull off than the project shown in FIGURE 1.9. The more shapes within a design, the more Bézier curves your art will have.

FIGURE 1.9 The raw Bézier curves for an illustration titled "Body & Soul." A complex illustration style like this one contains numerous vector shapes, and when viewed in its raw Bézier curve glory, can look pretty chaotic. But in reality, every anchor point and path is in its proper location.

FIGURE 1.10 Final "Body & Soul" illustration was created for a feature article in a women's health magazine.

FIGURE 1.11 What does this design lack? Answer: Straight lines. All of the raw vector paths within this tribal-styled design depend solely on Bézier curves to form the elegant shapes that make up the symmetrical design. (For more about symmetry see chapter 6.)

FIGURE 1.12 This design was created for an art showing in Mexico City.
I titled it "Nisqually" after the Indian tribe near the town where I grew up.

CHAPTER 2

Your Creative Armament

I've been creating vector artwork and wrangling with Bézier curves going on 18 years now. For 14 years, I was a die-hard Macromedia FreeHand user. Along the way, I'd use Adobe Illustrator from time to time—you know, if I *had* to. But when Adobe bought FreeHand, I saw the writing on the wall and committed myself to an exclusive relationship with Illustrator. We haven't always gotten along, Illustrator and me, but our marriage continues to deepen and improve with each passing software release.

A Love-Hate Relationship

It's hard to use something day in and day out—especially something so closely tied to my personal passion for design and creativity—without becoming somewhat fanatical about it. Let me start by saying that I *love* how Adobe Illustrator makes it so easy for me to turn my designs into precise, well-built vector illustrations.

However, as much as I appreciate Illustrator's many, many fine qualities, there are times when it drives me absolutely nuts. (Some of you may be nodding your heads in agreement.) Years ago, I wrote a blog post about my "switcher" frustrations and in the process coined the phrase "Adobe Frustrator." (You can see the post at http://snipurl.com/vonsterswitch.) Adobe's lead marketing director for Illustrator saw my post, agreed with many of my criticisms, and invited me to be on the Illustrator beta team. I've been part of that team since the release of Illustrator CS3 and have consulted on a handful of potential tools. So, as you can see, I've been watching the software's development for a long time.

After several years working with Illustrator and contributing to its development as a beta tester, I still have some big gripes about several of Illustrator's shortcomings, and I'll touch on these throughout this chapter. That said, the program has much improved since I first started using it and I have to admit that Adobe Illustrator is the best professional application for creating precise vector graphics in our industry. Hands down.

As a former die-hard FreeHand user for 14 years, you can be sure that I do not say these words lightly.

That said, whether you use Adobe Illustrator, CorelDraw, Inkscape—or any other app from an ever-growing list of open source vector drawing programs—before you can control Bézier curves and build vector art successfully, you must become familiar with your core building tools. All of these programs use Bézier curves for vector building. Every vector drawing program gives you the ability to build shapes via anchor points and paths. The difference among programs lies in the additional proprietary tools provided to manipulate points and paths.

For ease of communication, this book uses Adobe Illustrator to show-case the creative process. In this chapter, I'll tell you about the 12 core Illustrator tools you'll need to use to build precise vector graphics. If you don't have Illustrator, 11 of these tools have equivalents in the other vec-tor drawing programs. The few exceptions are the Xtream Path plug-in (www.cvalley.com) and the BetterHandles plug-in (http://www.nineblock.com), which were created specifically for Illustrator.

Vector building can be accomplished in any vector drawing program. The tools may have different names and might not work exactly the same way, but they should all enable you to arrive at the same precise solution. The key to success as an illustrative designer is to get back to basics. A sound and systematic creative process that includes analog drawing at its core will improve any designer's ability to execute digital art at a higher level.

Core Tools for Vector Building

Illustrator is replete with an array of tools that grows with each new soft-ware release. Whole books are dedicated to documenting these new tools and how to use them. This book, however, is dedicated to "basic training," so we'll only cover the 12 core tools needed to create precise vector shapes within any given drawing program.

The 12 Disciples of Design

Each of the 12 tools listed here serves a specific function in the build process. Keep in mind that some of these tools lend themselves to spe-cific build methods, which we'll go over in more detail in Chapter 6.

The 12 core tools you'll use to create precise vector shapes are:

1. **Pen tool** (P): Simply put, precise vector building wouldn't be pos-sible without the Pen tool. You'll use it to lay down all of your anchor points, one by one, forming a path that makes the vector shape you need (FIGURE 2.1).

2. **Add Anchor Point tool** (+): This tool allows you to add an additional anchor point to any path you have created (FIGURE 2.2).

3. **Delete Anchor Point tool** (–): This tool will remove any anchor point from any path you've created without breaking the path (FIGURE 2.3). I have a beef with this tool. You really shouldn't need it. This is a case of Illustrator making my life harder than it needs to be. We can only hope that the next version of Illustrator will allow you to simply highlight an anchor point and hit Delete—no special tool required to make it happen.

You can also select your anchor points and click "Remove selected anchor points" from the Control panel menu at the top of your screen. The results are the same.

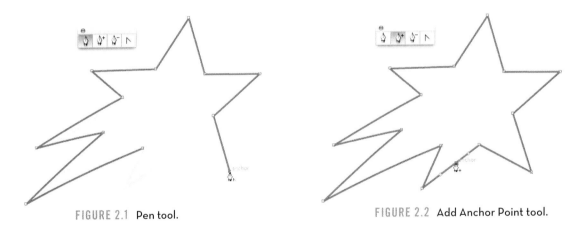

FIGURE 2.1 Pen tool.

FIGURE 2.2 Add Anchor Point tool.

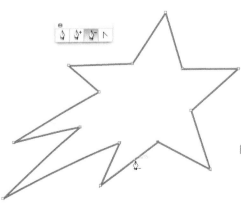

FIGURE 2.3 Delete Anchor Point tool.

4. **Convert Anchor Point tool** (Shift-C): This tool converts smooth points to corner points. It can also reveal, isolate, manipulate, and/or retract handlebars independently to adjust a Bézier curve (**FIGURE 2.4**).

5. **Selection tool** (V): Use this tool to scale objects larger or smaller. It also allows you to click or drag to select shapes as individual objects, and you can use it to manipulate handlebars to adjust a Bézier curve (**FIGURE 2.5**).

6. **Direct Selection tool** (A): This tool lets you directly click or drag to select a specific segment of a path or individual anchor points. It can also reveal, isolate, and manipulate handlebars to adjust a Bézier curve (**FIGURE 2.6**).

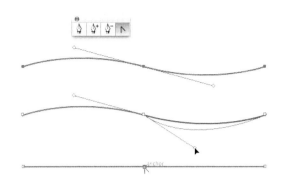

FIGURE 2.4 **Convert Anchor Point tool.**

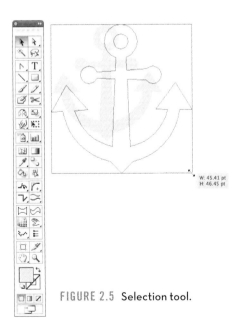

FIGURE 2.5 **Selection tool.**

FIGURE 2.6 **Direct Selection tool.**

7. **Rectangle tool** (M): This tool will create complete shapes with 90-degree angles (FIGURE 2.7). For more information, see "Shape Building Method" in Chapter 6.

8. **Ellipse tool** (L): This tool will create complete circular or elliptical shapes (FIGURE 2.8). For more information, see "Shape Building Method" in Chapter 6.

9. **Pathfinder tool** (Shift-Command-F9 or Shift-Control-F9): This tool enables you to create using shape-building techniques (think cookie cutters) using the tool's Unite, Minus Front, Intersect, and Exclude modes (FIGURES 2.9A–2.9D). There are other functions within the tool, but we'll only focus on these four shape modes.

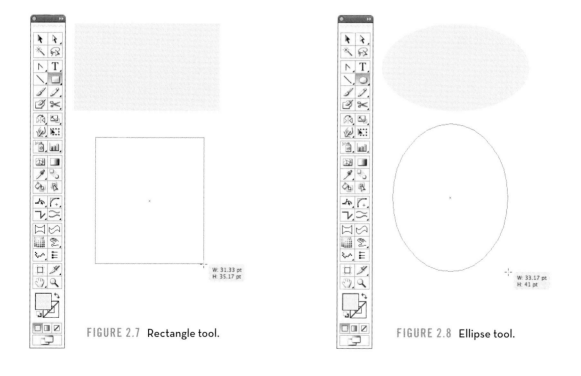

W: 31.33 pt
H: 35.17 pt

FIGURE 2.7   Rectangle tool.

W: 33.17 pt
H: 41 pt

FIGURE 2.8   Ellipse tool.

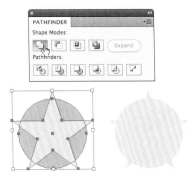

FIGURE 2.9A Pathfinder's Unite shape mode, before and after.

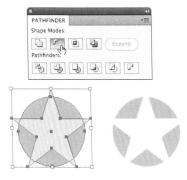

FIGURE 2.9B Pathfinder's Minus Front shape mode, before and after.

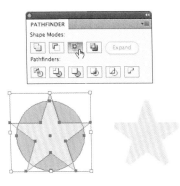

FIGURE 2.9C Pathfinder's Intersect shape mode, before and after.

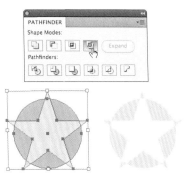

FIGURE 2.9D Pathfinder's Exclude shape mode, before and after. Personally, I never use this function.

10. **Rotate tool** (R): This tool allows you to define the rotating axis of any selected object and rotate it on the fly or via a specific numerical amount (**FIGURE 2.10**).

11. **Reflect tool** (O): With this tool, flip a selected object either horizontally or vertically. You'll use it mainly for creating symmetrical designs (**FIGURE 2.11**). For more information, see "Symmetry Is Your Friend" in Chapter 6.

12. **Xtream Path plug-in** (CValley Software): This plug-in makes editing and forming your final vector shapes far easier and more precise than Adobe's own tools (Warp tool, Shift-R). The plug-in comes with many useful tools, but we'll focus specifically on the Segment Direct Edit tool, Symmetric Edit tool, Round Fillet tool, and a drop-down menu object filter it adds called Smart Rounding (**FIGURE 2.12**).

FIGURE 2.10 **Rotate tool.**

FIGURE 2.11 **Reflect tool.**

FIGURE 2.12 **Xtream Path plug-in's Segment Direct Edit tool, Symmetric Edit tool, Round Fillet tool, and the Smart Rounding filter.**

Xtream Path Plug-in

When I first discovered the Xtream Path plug-in, I knew I had found the Holy Grail of vector building. It has not only made creating vector art within Illustrator easier and more precise, but it's also proven to be a far superior build method to anything I used to know and love in FreeHand.

FreeHand made editing anchor points and paths easier than Adobe Illustrator did, with fewer tools, less hassle, and in less time. When I switched to Adobe Illustrator, my build time slowed down. The Xtream Path plug-in simplified the Illustrator process with one tool, no hassle, and resulted in a faster build time than either FreeHand or Illustrator provided. Should you use the Xtream Path plug-in? It's a no-brainer.

The Xtream Path plug-in is a superior tool for editing and shaping vector graphics. The plug-in is well worth the investment (about $140) because the time you'll save in frustration-free building will more than cover the cost.

The Three Amigos, Plus One

The Xtream Path plug-in is made up of 33 individual tools, but we will use three of these and one drop-down menu in this book. They are:

1. **Segment Direct Edit tool:** This tool allows you to literally grab a vector path anywhere (between two anchor points) and bend it into any freeform shape (**FIGURE 2.13**).

FIGURE 2.13 Grab a vector path anywhere between two anchor points and bend the Bézier curve into the specific shape needed to match your drawing. You'll simply push and pull your paths to form them into your final art (like vector clay, if you will). The functionality is simple, intuitive, and, most importantly, leads to precise vector building.

2. **Symmetric Edit tool:** With this tool, you can grab a path (between two anchor points) and symmetrically distort it evenly in the direction in which you are moving the path (**FIGURE 2.14**).

3. **Round Fillet tool:** This tool allows you to drag over independent anchor points and visually round them off on the fly, or you can round off points to an exact specification that you set in the Control panel. It only works on corner anchor points that have no Bézier curves pulled out (**FIGURE 2.15**).

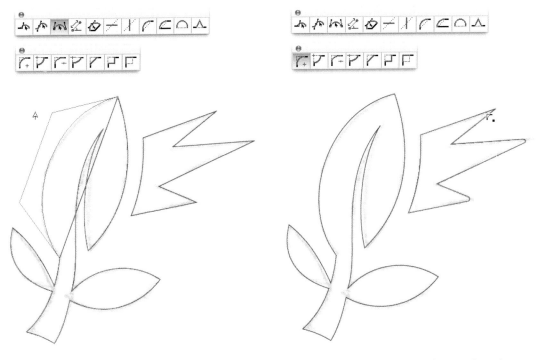

FIGURE 2.14 Evenly distort a path with mathematical precision using the Symmetric Edit tool.

FIGURE 2.15 Simple, on-the-fly rounding of vector shapes using the Round Fillet tool.

4. **Smart Rounding filter:** This useful filter allows you to select a whole object or just an individual anchor point and round it off—regardless if the path has a Bézier curve on it or not. To access the Smart Rounding filter, select Object > Filters > Xtream Path > Smart Rounding (**FIGURE 2.16**). You can also use the Smart Rounding filter to round off any type of path regardless of anchor point types. Either select the whole shape or individual anchor points.

FIGURE 2.16 Round off any type of path with the Smart Rounding filter.

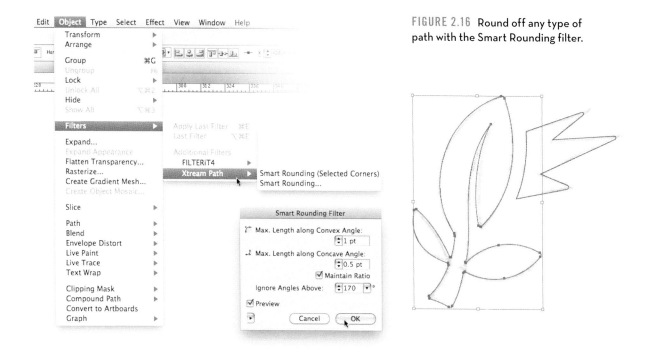

Customize Your Environment

Every vector drawing program comes with default settings. In general, the defaults are OK, but customizing your preferences will make creating your vector graphics a lot easier. The following customizations are geared for Adobe Illustrator. Look for equivalent controls and features in the drawing application of your choice.

My Preference for Preferences

You'll want to customize these three areas.

1. **Preferences/General:** The settings shown in FIGURE 2.17 will help you make adjustments to your art as you work and scale properly when resizing.

2. **Preferences/Selection and Anchor Display:** The settings shown in FIGURE 2.18 will make it easier for you to notice and isolate problem areas in your vector shapes. They will also assist you in editing and adjusting your anchor points, their handles, and Bézier curves as you build.

FIGURE 2.17 Preferences > General: Keep Keyboard Increment set at 1 point or lower. Make sure you have Scale Strokes & Effects checked.

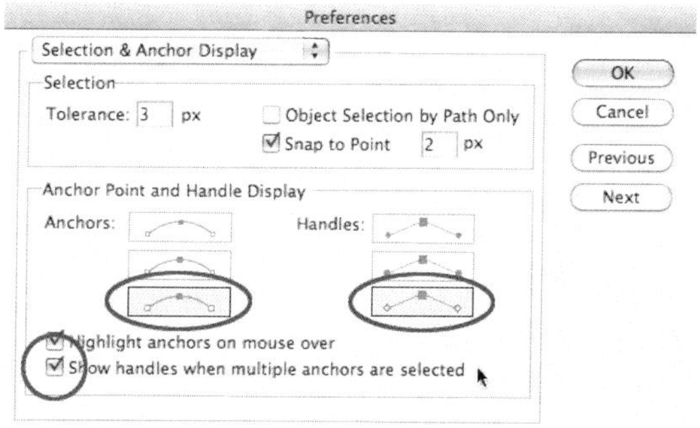

FIGURE 2.18 Preferences > Selection & Anchor Display: Select the largest display for your "Anchors" and "Handles" by choosing the last, largest box featuring the handles that have the hollow ends. Make sure you have Show handles when multiple anchors are selected checked.

3. **Preferences/Smart Guides:** The settings shown in FIGURE 2.19 will enable the
assistance of Smart Guides as you build.
This will help you know when you're hover-
ing over an anchor point in a path that isn't
selected, for example.

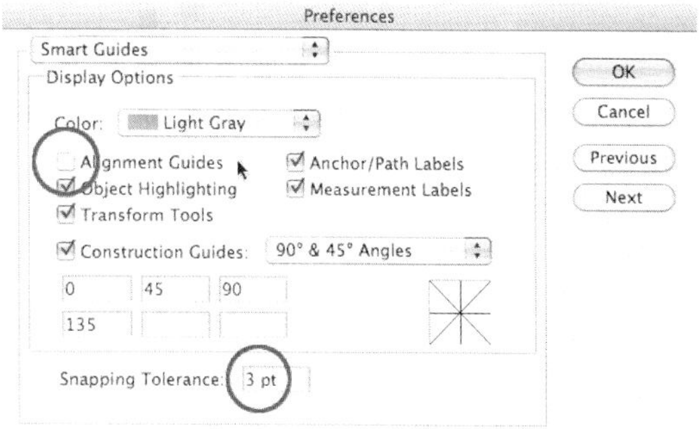

Keyboard Shortcuts and Actions

The ability to customize your own keyboard
commands and create actions in Adobe Illustrator are, in my opinion, two of Illustrator's
most underrated features. Most people never
even tap into them.

FIGURE 2.19 Preferences > Smart Guides: Make
sure you have Alignment Guides unchecked. And set
your Snapping Tolerance to 3 pt. or lower. I uncheck
Alignment Guides because the program tries to
associate everything you build with other elements
in your file whether you want it to or not, and this can
become highly annoying as you build vector shapes.

Keyboard shortcuts are just what they sound
like: the ability to use a key command instead
of hunting down the command in a pulldown
menu. They allow you to be more efficient.

Not all functions in Illustrator allow you to add a shortcut command,
though. In those cases, actions are your best bet. Actions allow you to
record multiple keyboard commands. Once you are done recording, you
can assign the recording to a specific key command. The end result is
that with one push of a key, you can run a series of commands instantly,
which obviously saves time. The best way to determine how you can
best use actions is to simply experiment. Anything you do routinely is a
good candidate for an action.

To create your own keyboard shortcuts, go to Edit > Keyboard Shortcuts > Select, and pick either Tools or Menu Command from the
pulldown menu in the pop-up window. Select a specific tool or menu
command, and then enter in the key you want the task to be assigned to.
Illustrator will tell you if the key is already assigned, and you can decide
to ignore or override it. Click Save, and your keyboard shortcut is ready
to use. It's that simple.

To create an action, go to Window > Actions. On the Actions panel, click the fly-out menu in the top-right corner. Then click New Action. In the pop-up window that opens, name your action, assign it to an action set, assign a key command to it, and click Record > Proceed to compile the series of commands you want to record (see Figure 2.20). (Remember that not all functions in Illustrator are recordable.) Once done, click Stop in the Actions palette. You now have a customized action at the ready.

How you ultimately use these features will depend greatly on what type of work you'll be creating, but when it comes to building vector graphics, I have customized a handful of commands to make routine tasks easier. Here are six shortcuts and two actions that I use regularly via my F keys to save time.

1. **F1** is Make Clipping Mask (Command-7 or Control-7).

2. **F2** is Release Clipping Mask (Option-Command-7 or Alt-Control-7).

3. **F3** is Clone. Adobe Illustrator has no clone command. To clone an object, you must copy a shape (Command-C or Control-C) and then paste it in front (Command-F or Control-F). That's a total of four keys to hit. Keyboard shortcuts don't allow multiple commands, so you'll need to record an action and assign the action to the specific F key you want (**FIGURE 2.20**).

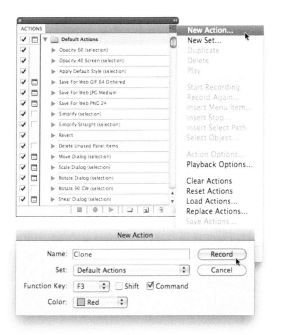

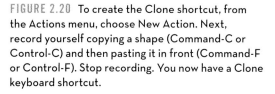

FIGURE 2.20 **To create the Clone shortcut, from the Actions menu, choose New Action. Next, record yourself copying a shape (Command-C or Control-C) and then pasting it in front (Command-F or Control-F). Stop recording. You now have a Clone keyboard shortcut.**

4. **F4** is Send to Back (Shift-Command-[or Shift-Control={).

5. **F5** is Bring to Front Again (Shift-Command-] or Shift-Control-]).

6. **F6** is Ungroup (Shift-Command-G or Shift-Control-G).

7. **F7** is Unite. This allows me to take two selected shapes and unite them into one shape without having to move my cursor to the Pathfinder panel. In Adobe Illustrator CS5, the Shape Building tool (Shift-M) could be assigned to this F key, if you want.

   Since the Pathfinder panel functions don't have keyboard commands, I created an action for this function and assigned the action to the F7 key.

8. **F8** is Deselect (Shift-Command-A or Shift-Control-A). Sometimes when you're zoomed into your design, you can't click on the artboard to deselect an object. Assigning the Deselect shortcut to the F8 key is like killing three keys with one click.

Stop Re-creating the Wheel

When you begin a new project, you should be able to start building immediately. Your creative process shouldn't waste a bunch of time setting preferences, importing your styles and color swatches, creating new layer structures, and so on at the start of each and every project. I save myself a ton of time and frustration by creating a new document profile in Illustrator that saves many of my favorite settings and uses them as the default settings for each document.

In this section, I'll show you how to set the foundation for a creative process that enables you to spend less time fussing with your computer and more time creating great designs.

Create a New Document Profile

Creating a new document profile in Illustrator is a simple three-step process.

1. **Create a new document** (Command-N or Control-N). In the New Document dialog, select the general properties you want, name the file, and click OK (**FIGURE 2.21**).

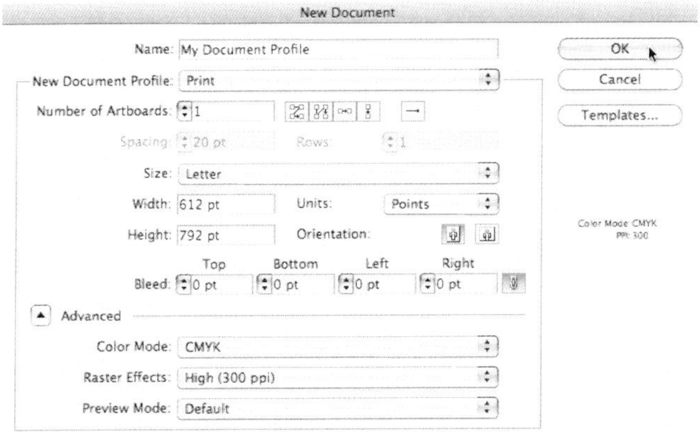

FIGURE 2.21 Many of the settings in the New Document window will be determined by the specific project you're working on. If you overlook something after you click OK, don't worry. You can always go back and revise it as needed.

2. **Customize your properties.** In your new document, set up properties in the way you like to work. Maybe you prefer rules to always be visible, specific colors to be loaded in your swatches panel, and so on. It's up to you. (We'll go over three essential properties that you should include in your new document profile in "Set Graphic Styles for Building" later in this chapter.)

3. **Save your startup profile** (Command-S or Control-S). Once you have your file set up with all the properties you want it to contain, it's time to save it. Go to File > Save (Command-S or Control-S) and save your startup profile in this location: User/Library/Application Support/Adobe/Adobe Illustrator Version/Language/New Document Profiles.

From this point forward, your new profile will appear in the New Document dialog (**FIGURE 2.22**). You can simply select it and get straight to work.

A fringe benefit of working within a systematic creative process is that it removes a lot of guesswork. When you approach a new project using your customized new document profile, you can focus on the creative

FIGURE 2.22 This is how your startup profile is listed in the New Document dialog.

work rather than the tools needed to pull it off. Being consistent will help you be more efficient and allow you to spend more time on actual creative work rather than file management.

There are other ways to speed up your vector build times as well, and we'll get to those next.

Set Graphic Styles for Building

Two primary tasks define the creative process described in this book: drawing and building. You'll draw out your art, scan it in, and then build it within your vector drawing program. Drawing is the creative foundation upon which you build.

Prior to starting the building process, you'll want to create two simple graphic styles and save them in your new document profile. These determine your working line weight and color during the build process. To create a graphic style, just create any shape with any fill or stroke color and width you want, and drag it into the Graphic Styles palette. Done.

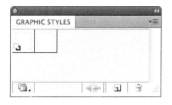

FIGURE 2.23 My default graphic style is a .5 pt. magenta colored stroke. I also have a secondary graphic style that is a .25 magenta-colored stroke. These help me easily see what I am creating.

When I scan in a drawing that will form the basis of a digital illustration, the scan shows up in black and white and then is grayed back for building. By setting my default line styles in magenta, the colored lines pop off the background and I can clearly see what I'm creating. The color you choose doesn't have to be magenta—that's just *my* personal preference. Use whatever color you want as long as it's not black, which would be too hard to see (FIGURE 2.23).

As you build your vector art, you'll zoom in and out so you can see certain portions better. When I'm zoomed out, I use the .5 pt. stroke, and when I'm zoomed in I use the .25 pt. stroke (FIGURE 2.23). Using a .5 pt. stroke when zoomed in produces a line that's too fat, which makes it hard to analyze contoured shapes as you build. Using a .25 pt. stroke when zoomed out does the opposite: The line is too thin and hard to see.

Enable Smart Guides for Building

I highly recommend that you enable Smart Guides (Command-U or Control-U) as you build your artwork. Smart Guides make snapping to points and paths more obvious, and without them, it's easy to think something is snapped into the correct location, only to find out later that it's slightly off.

Smart Guides will also help you select items with more precision and assist you with live pop-up information when you rotate items or hover over content in your document (FIGURE 2.24).

Using Smart Guides is a balancing act, however. I find myself toggling them on and off throughout the creative process because sometimes they can get in the way or force a snap when you don't want it.

If you're not used to working with these guides turned on, I suggest you get used to it. The benefits outweigh the annoying GUI behavior.

Establish a Layer Structure for Building

For whatever reason, Adobe has decided that layer information isn't worthy of being one of the properties you can add to a new document profile. This is highly annoying and should be added to a future version of the software, in my humble opinion.

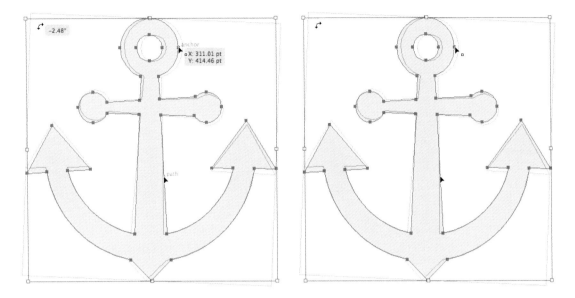

FIGURE 2.24 Left: With Smart Guides enabled, you can select a point or path, or rotate a selected object. Also, Smart Guides will give you immediate information. The information displayed by Smart Guides changes based on the tools you are using and what shapes you happen to mouse over as you work. Right: With Smart Guides turned off, a selected point, path, or rotated object displays no information.

For now, we have to establish layers manually. Whether I'm working on a logo design, character illustration, or a pattern design, I follow the same hierarchy when it comes to layering during my building stage (FIGURE 2.25). I start with four layers: storage, temporary, build, and scan.

From the top down, my layers are as follows:

1. **Storage Layer:** As I build artwork, I tend to experiment. So I make copies of elements and move them to my storage layer, which is not visible. I also make a copy of all of my paths before I start coloring and put those in the storage layer as well. Think of this approach as vector insurance in case you mess something up. It also allows me to more easily take elements I may have created for one project and reuse them in another.

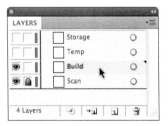

FIGURE 2.25 I begin every project with four layers: a storage layer, temporary layer, build layer, and scan layer.

Bézier Curve Jedi Master

Do not be intimidated by the systematic creative process, new methods, or new tools we'll tackle in this book, my Padawan learner.

Think of your vector drawing program as your design lightsaber. How well you wield it will determine how precise your final vector artwork turns out. Let the creative force flow through you. I'll play the part of a little green Muppet.

Yes, there is a lot to master. But master you must.

"Try not. Do or do not, there is no try." — Yoda

2. **Temp Layer:** I use this layer to test things before I actually make them part of the build art. The more I build, the more a file can get cluttered visually, so this allows me the space to turn off the other layers and work on a clean surface. Once I have the specific vector art dialed in, I then move it to the build layer.

3. **Build Layer:** This is where most of my building takes place. It serves as my vector staging ground on which to construct the vector artwork and finesse my Bézier curves.

4. **Scan Layer:** This is where I place my refined drawing scan (either a .tif or .psd file with transparency set to around 20). I then lock the layer so it cannot move.

As a project progresses from building the core vector graphics, and I begin the process of coloring and detailing the artwork, I'll add additional layers to make managing and editing the artwork easier. We'll cover this in more detail in Chapter 9.

DESIGN DRILLS:
Deconstructing Design

All professional designers and illustrators practice good layer management, and you should, too. In fact, you'll want to set up an established layer structure for each and every vector art file that you create.

Organize and group related content on its own layer as you build, and you'll be able to isolate a specific group easily when edits are needed down the road. And, I assure you, edits will be needed. They always are. Grouping related content by layers allows you to make adjustments faster and refine details in your design without other vector shapes getting in your way.

Let's deconstruct two of my designs. By turning the layers on and off, you'll be able to see how the vector content is organized.

Señor Skully

This design was originally created for a sticker manufacturer, but the client changed directions. So, I turned it into a Day of the Dead poster (FIGURES 2.26–2.30).

FIGURE 2.26 These two layers, part of a poster design, host the background content.

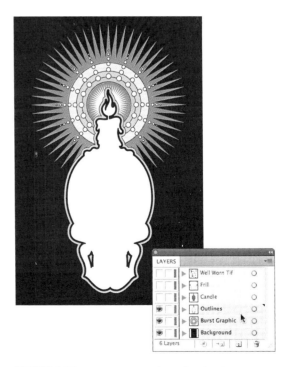

FIGURE 2.27 Keeping my outlines for this design on their own layer makes experimenting with the stroke thickness much easier.

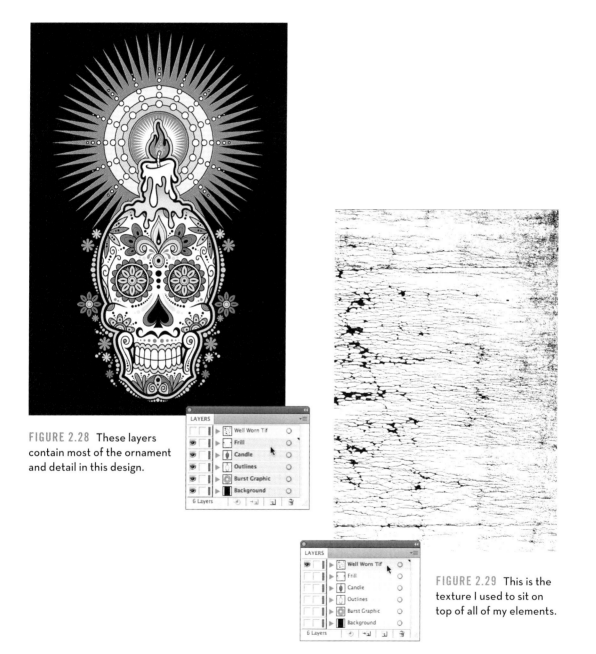

FIGURE 2.28 These layers contain most of the ornament and detail in this design.

FIGURE 2.29 This is the texture I used to sit on top of all of my elements.

FIGURE 2.30 Final Day of the Dead poster design.

Loyal Order of Wormwood

Adobe gave me complete creative freedom to design a poster to help market CS4 Illustrator. My twisted mind came up with this fun design.

FIGURE 2.31 These five layers make up the background elements and texturing for a poster design.

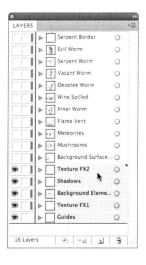

FIGURE 2.32 These six layers hold the secondary illustrative elements.

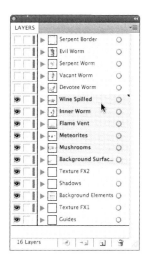

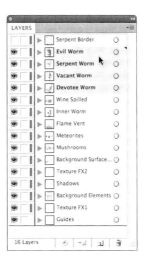

FIGURE 2.33 These four layers flesh out the entire interior illustration of my design.

FIGURE 2.34 The top layer contains the illustrative frame for this design.

FIGURE 2.35 The title of this poster is "Loyal Order of Wormwood." You can find the original Ai file for this design within the Cool Extras folder included with either CS4 or CS5 Adobe Illustrator.

CHAPTER 3

Analog Methods in a Digital Age

I, a designer of Planet Earth, in order to form a more perfect creative process, establish drawing skills, ensure design tranquility, provide excellent art, promote conceptual welfare, and secure the blessings of creative liberty to ourselves and our posterity, do ordain and establish this chapter for the designers of our world.

Don't Be a Tooler

I graduated from art school in 1986. Even though the program was specifically geared for training graphic designers, we had to take drawing and illustration classes regardless of if we ever wanted to become professional illustrators. At the time, our industry fully realized the importance of drawing as it relates to design.

But times have changed. Most art schools that offer visual communications degrees don't require students to take any drawing classes. The majority focus on software-oriented design (a tool-driven process), which only compounds the problem.

This issue isn't relegated to the realm of just recent design school graduates, however. Even seasoned designers who have been trained to draw have sometimes been lulled into creative torpor by the ease and accessibility of digital tools as well, either occasionally or permanently.

This dumbing down of creativity in our industry is a serious pet peeve of mine. Those who bake down the creative process so it's not too demanding on the individual believe the computer and not the artist is the wellspring of creativity.

The fundamental problem for many designers is the lack of a well-defined and systematic creative process. In today's design reality, it's far too easy to fall into the routine of jumping on the computer as the first step in a creative task. We've all been guilty of this at one time or another. But any designer who jumps directly onto the computer is what I would call a "tooler."

A tooler is someone who doesn't necessarily want to improve his or her drawing skills, but who thinks that by learning the latest software version, or applying a new pull-down menu effect, or running a filter in a certain way, or mimicking some other type of convoluted Fibonacchi-esque computer process, he or she will be able to actually skirt drawing.

Toolers don't draw. In making that choice, they not only lessen the quality of the final product, but they also fail to grow as designers. It's a lose-lose situation.

Analog—that is, drawing—and digital are not independent of each other when it comes to creating artwork. Nothing I do is fully digital, nor is it fully analog. I'm constantly going back and forth between the two throughout the creative process.

I Get Paid to Draw

Early in my career (pre-computer), people would ask me what I did for a living and I'd say, "I'm a graphic designer." The usual response was something like, "You get paid to draw? I can't draw a stick figure," and they'd proceed to admire, recognize, and clearly associate my core skill and craft with what I did for a living.

But now (post-computer) when I tell people what I do, the normal response tends to be something like this: "That's cool. I have a computer, too. I printed some inkjet business cards for..." And they proceed to associate what they do on a hack PC in their spare time using Microsoft Paint, prefab templates, Comic Sans font, and clip-art with what I do as a professional for a living.

Gone is the appreciation or even recognition of a skill or craft we as artists possess to do our jobs. For the most part, toolers don't view themselves as lacking any core ability as "designers" because the computer, in their minds has replaced the skill and craft they once associated with an artist's ability.

Our industry is now inundated with toolers who reinforce this poor public perception of what we do. Toolers don't take skill and craft seriously. In essence, one could argue that they are merely glorified amateurs who just know more about the software than the general public. Mom and Pop see what they produce and say to themselves, "Hey, I can do that, too." And thus the tooler dispensation was born.

As I stated in the introduction of this chapter, I don't expect every designer to be a full-blown illustrator, but I do think every designer should integrate basic drawing skills into the creative process in order to create to his or her fullest potential (FIGURE 3.1). This chapter will help you understand the importance of working your ideas out in analog form before moving to digital—that is, working your ideas out on paper before ever approaching the computer.

FIGURE 3.1 **Stop looking for ideas in pulldown menus and start improving your analog drawing skills.**

Concepts and Ideas

I teach digital illustration at a local college, and I tell all of my students on the first day of class that I cannot teach them to be creative. I can only show them methods that will aid them in their quest to create and execute unique concepts and ideas.

A tome could be written on the subject of idea generation and how someone uses creative thinking and mental problem solving within a design context. Suffice it to say that this book is geared to facilitate the execution of your ideas and not the creation of them.

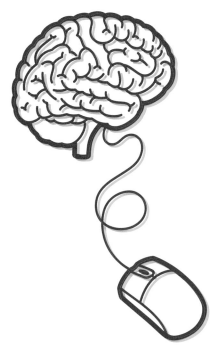

Every creative process has a beginning. A solid creative foundation starts with research, knowing your audience, and thinking through ideas that are appropriate for that audience both strategically and aesthetically. Only then can you begin to draw.

Your brain is the only computer you need at this point. You're mining, not refining, so it's important to load the chamber (your brain) with as much relevant information as you can in order to fuel your creative exploration as you draw out your ideas (FIGURE 3.2).

FIGURE 3.2 **Everyone has a potential super computer sitting in-between his or her shoulders. Load that computer with as much information as possible so you can draw on it when needed (pun intended).**

Analog Tools

As I draw out my ideas and work through the creative process, there are three main tools I depend upon every day (**FIGURE 3.3**):

1. 2B pencil for roughing out concepts and chewing on.

2. Ballpoint pen to quickly create thumbnail sketches.

3. Mechanical pencil for drawing out my refined sketches, which I then scan and build upon in my vector drawing program.

I also like to use a black Sharpie and a red pen as I work, but those don't play a part in the foundational stage of my creative process. I use them in refining my artwork, as you'll see later.

The Lost Art of Thumbnailing

I love the term "thumbnailing." It's an apropos term to define the capturing of ideas in a simple and small (thumbnail-sized) drawing. Because you're just mining for concepts at this point, you don't need to worry about how precise or technically accurate the image is. Thumbnails are nothing more than visual triggers to help you explore the creative possibilities.

Think of the process as "brain dumping." You're simply opening up the floodgates of your mind and letting the ideas flow out on to paper. Have fun with the process: Don't get hung up on how appropriate the concept is at this point or how good the sketches are. You'll go through and refine your direction later.

You could also refer to these as doodles. In reality, the only difference between a traditional doodle and a thumbnail sketch is that one tends to be purposeful and the other merely spontaneous or random, lacking a focused intent. But if calling these sketches "doodles" takes the pressure off, then go for it.

An aside: As much as I try to specifically plan for a project, I never know when inspiration will hit me. Many times something I see or think will

FIGURE 3.3 If the pen is mightier than the sword, then it's a safe bet the mouse is no match for it either.

trigger an idea and I'll grab a pen and whatever paper is handy to thumbnail the concept out and just capture the idea. This is why you'll see different ink and paper colors in my thumbnail sketches (**FIGURE 3.4**).

Thumbnails may start out very crude, but through a process of refinement they lead to well-crafted and precise digital artwork (**FIGURE 3.5**).

FIGURE 3.4
Thumbnails-o-plenty.

FIGURE 3.5 Thumbnailing forms the foundation for any type of creative project, be it pattern design, custom lettering, character design, tribal illustration, icon design, or a logo mark.

More Is Better

You can never have too many thumbnails, but you can have too few. Always push yourself to create more than what you need for any given project. This will ensure you've fully vetted your exploration.

> "Nothing is more dangerous than an idea when it is the only one you have."   — ÉMILE CHARTIER

There's a nice fringe benefit to over-thumbnailing: Over time, you'll build an archive of "homeless" ideas. When a new project comes along that aligns with a previous project's theme, you can harvest ideas from your unused archive. It's like renewable creative energy!

An Exception to the Rule

That said, there are exceptions. Not all projects need lots of thumbnails. Sometimes the design motif is iconic and simple and you don't need to refine it beyond your initial thumbnail sketch.

A creative process should be flexible enough to allow this approach without compromising the end results. It obviously won't apply to every job you work on, but in the case of my "Freedom of Speech" project, it did (FIGURE 3.6). The speech bubble element was clearly going to be an "easy-to-build" object (FIGURE 3.7).

This project was built primarily using basic shapes within my drawing program. In essence, why try to draw a perfect elliptical shape when there's a tool that already does it with precision? This applies to the star shape as well.

FIGURE 3.6 My concept was a very graphic and stylized speaking bubble that also read as an eagle.

FIGURE 3.7 Final "Freedom of Speech" design.

This project is, of course, the exception, not the rule. More often than not you'll want to thumbnail out your ideas and then redraw and refine before trying to pull off the vector artwork.

Refine Your Drawing

Before you'd get into your car and drive somewhere you'd never been to before, you'd likely check a map for directions. If you didn't bother getting a map, you'd probably get lost, drive a route that was not very efficient, and experience a lot of frustration trying to figure things out on the fly.

The same is true when it comes to building vector artwork. Drawing out and refining your ideas will give you a precise road map that you can then follow within your vector drawing program. It removes the guess-work out of building your art (FIGURE 3.8).

But if you don't take the time to think through and draw what you need to build before you build it, you'll waste a lot of time noodling around looking for that result you're after. If in doubt, redraw on paper.

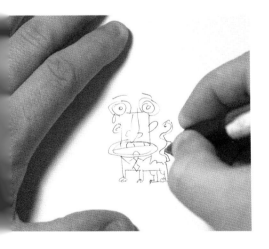

Refinement is a process of evolving your art from a rough idea into a clari-fied plan from which you can build.

But if something just doesn't look right after redrawing your art as you refine it, then it's a good bet you need to rework it more. Whenever you're in doubt about how your drawing looks, redraw it (FIGURE 3.9).

Refinement isn't a task reserved for just this stage of the creative process: it should blanket the whole process. A smart designer will learn to art direct him- or herself over time and make continual refinements along the way (FIGURE 3.10).

FIGURE 3.8 Thumbnail sketch for character design.

I find it a lot easier to draw on vellum and use a light box. I usually only redraw the parts of a drawing that I don't like and then just tape the various "right" parts together to form the final refined sketch that I can scan.

This process takes dedication. If you're not used to working this way, it will seem foreign, but hang in there. Over time it will get easier, and you'll get better at it.

You may invest more time upfront, but in the long run it will save you even more time, expand your creative skill sets, and produce better work.

FIGURE 3.9 A more refined version of my original thumbnail, shown on the previous page.

FIGURE 3.10 Final refined sketch I'll now use as my road map to build upon in my vector drawing program.

Create a Better Road Map

Have you ever tried to follow a map that wasn't accurate? It kind of defeats the purpose. The same is true when you draw out your refined artwork. The more precise it is, the easier it will be to build it in vector form. Once you're happy with your drawing, you can scan it into your vector drawing program.

The following project is one that shows how to build an accurate road map (FIGURES 3.11–3.14). Its earlier thumbnails are shown on the two previous pages.

FIGURE 3.11 This more refined version is closer to what I need but it still could be improved upon. The amount of time you'd spend finessing vectors would take more time than just redrawing it in a more precise form on paper.

FIGURE 3.12 All guesswork has been removed. You now have a clear road map of where to place your points and how your vector paths should be built.

FIGURE 3.13 My refined final sketch has enabled me to build my artwork with precision. In other words, analog equips digital to be more effective.

FIGURE 3.14 Final precise vector artwork of my character design. (Kanji: Create!)

This sketch-and-refine process can apply to any type of design project that needs to end up in vector form. In this example, we're showcasing a custom hand-lettered logotype design (**FIGURES 3.15–3.21**).

FIGURE 3.15 A thumbnail sketch establishes a direction for my logotype design.

FIGURE 3.16 Rough sketching and refining my concept. I'm not worrying about precise shapes at this point; I'm just trying to flesh out the look and feel and balance the weight of the letterforms and negative space.

FIGURE 3.17 I start drawing out my refined sketch. I'm now thinking about vector shapes. How will I go about building this in vector form? Drawing my art precisely in analog facilitates the building of it in digital.

FIGURE 3.18 Final refined sketch ready to scan in and place in my drawing application.

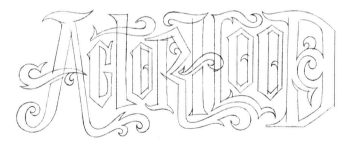

FIGURE 3.19 Using my refined drawing as my road map to build my vector shapes with precision.

FIGURE 3.20 I print out my concept and, using a Sharpie, I experiment with various details. Once I have my art tweaks nailed down, I'll reference it and make the changes to my digital files. This is a good example of analog and digital working together.

FIGURE 3.21 Final custom logotype design.

Back and Forth

DVD ▶ Here's another instance that illustrates why the analog-to-vector process is essential. For this project I had to illustrate a three-eyed monster in a pseudo woodcut style. To pull off this style, I had to go back and forth from digital to analog throughout its creation (**FIGURES 3.22–3.30**).

FIGURE 3.22 Thumbnail sketch for "Tri3ye Guy" illustration.

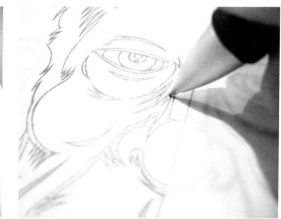

FIGURE 3.23 I drew out my vector shapes in a refined sketch before I built them.

FIGURE 3.24 My final refined sketch, ready to scan in. Since this illustration is symmetrical, I only have to draw out half of it in Illustrator. (More about symmetry in Chapter 6.)

FIGURE 3.25 No guesswork is needed as I build vector shapes. I simply follow what I've already predetermined in my refined sketch.

FIGURE 3.26 I print out my base black-and-white art and draw in how I want the shading to be built in vector form. I'll do this several times during a project in order to work out all of the detail in my illustration.

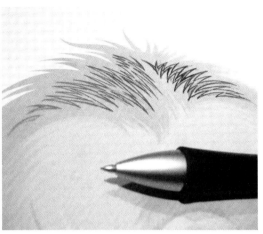

FIGURE 3.27 Here is a refined drawing of highlight detail in the figure's hair. I could have tried to render this without drawing it first, but it would have taken me a lot longer and probably not looked as good.

FIGURE 3.28 Using vellum, I draw on top of a color print-out using my light box to work out highlight details that I'll need to build out in vector form. This process of going back and forth from digital to analog becomes second nature over time.

FIGURE 3.29 This image shows a close-up of the vector detailing in this illustration.

FIGURE 3.30 Final Tri3ye Guy illustration.

Systematic and Creative

Designers create on behalf of clients. Our design solutions need to work professionally within a commercial environment. And our creative work has to fit with a client's business personality and marketing strategy. We also need to create artwork within a set budget and schedule, which means we don't have the luxury of spending as much time as we might like on any given project.

These are all reasons why a systematic creative process is necessary when creating vector-based artwork. Building your vector designs on a solid creative foundation is a must in order to produce work that is precise, on time, and effective.

The more you work systematically as you build vector artwork, the more the process becomes second nature and the faster you'll be able to execute your ideas without compromising the quality of the art.

Let's take a look at this systematic process in context of creating a more complex project: a brand logo development for a new line of clothing called "Beloved Virus" (**FIGURES 3.31–3.43**).

FIGURE 3.31 I helped conceive the name for this client's new business venture, so being able to then flesh out a visual representation of that name was a lot of fun. This shows a handful of the thumbnail concepts I sketched out.

FIGURE 3.32 I wanted the mark to be more timeless and less gimmicky, so I liked the idea of an ornate, hand-lettered typographic treatment. At this stage, I put meat on the bones of my idea and started defining the design. This gives me a good idea of what to expect, but it's still not good enough to build from.

FIGURE 3.33 I've now redrawn the letterforms more precisely with my mechanical pencil. I'm still scrutinizing the balance of the shapes and looking for areas I can refine even more.

FIGURE 3.34 I put the project aside for the day and approach it with fresh eyes the next morning when I find more room for improvement. I modify several letterforms and am now ready to create my final refined sketch.

FIGURE 3.35 On this specific project, I scanned in and printed out my rough at a larger size so I could redraw the final refined sketch with maximum precision.

FIGURE 3.36 I scan my final refined sketch and now have an exact road map from which to build my vector artwork upon. No guesswork will be involved; I already know what the logo should look like.

FIGURE 3.37 Whenever I build vector artwork, I form my art by creating smaller shapes. It's far easier than trying to create using one single shape. (Note: This and all of the build techniques demonstrated in this chapter will be explained in upcoming chapters.)

FIGURE 3.38 For example, look at the letter "B." It's made from eight different individual shapes. If I tried to build this as one or two shapes, it would be a major pain to get it built precisely. The end result wouldn't be as graceful or elegant either.

FIGURE 3.39 I continue using this same build method to create all of my letterforms for this design.

FIGURE 3.40 I call this simple method "shape building," and I'll go over it in more detail in Chapter 6.

FIGURE 3.41 I fuse all of my shapes together to form my base art for the brand logo.

FIGURE 3.42 Along the way, I distorted the perspective of my type treatment and nested it within a bolded outline shape. The end result is an effective, precision-built brand logo derived from the solid creative foundation of drawing.

FIGURE 3.43 The same systematic process was used to design and build all of the logo concepts I presented to my client.

If you've already determined that you can't do the drawing part of this process very well, then my book has taught you something already. You need to improve on your core drawing skills. That is what growing as a designer is all about.

I'm often asked, "How do I get better at drawing?" The answer is easy: You start drawing now, and you stick with it. If you started drawing today (doodling counts, by the way), in five years you'll be a lot better.

When is Drawing Done?

You draw out your thumbnail sketches, isolate a good idea, rough it out, redraw it, and refine it multiple times. It begs the question:

"How do you know when you're done drawing?"

The answer depends on the individual who is doing the drawing. If the drawing doesn't feel right, then you know you're not done refining it. When I say "feel," I literally mean it. It's a second-sense type of thing. You just get to a point where you know it looks right.

If something is bugging you about your drawing, then it's a good bet you need to redraw something. Stepping away from your project and approaching it with "fresh eyes" later will help you see where you can make improvements.

We'll cover this in more depth in Chapter 8.

One of the coolest aspects of a creative career is our talent and skill don't diminish over time. Like wine, they only get better with age. But if you never start, you'll never improve.

The whole idea behind drawing out your vector art before you build it is to create a piece of digital art that is precise and well-crafted. Your final art will just come out better.

But if that wasn't enough, vector artwork is resolution independent, which means that you can use it in almost any format or application once it has been created in vector form. It extends your design's possibilities.

I've shown you the importance of drawing out your ideas and refining them, but you've only seen a glimpse of the actual vector build methods you'll use in your vector drawing program once your drawing is complete.

You may be saying to yourself at this point, "I can draw out my ideas, but actually building the vector art is a major pain in the ass."

Fear not, my weary friend! The next three chapters will demystify vector building through simple systematic methods that will equip you for vector success.

DESIGN DRILLS:
Essential Nonsense

I'd never say that I completely understand all of my own doodles because I don't. Most just flow out of me without any forethought. I simply open up the floodgates and see what happens. It's more fun that way.

I'll admit most are strange, and some are a bit disturbing. The latter category I refer to as, "Dark Morsels." Once again, don't ask me what they mean because I'd be guessing, just like you.

That said, I think doodling is a great way to exercise creatively. That's why I consider doodling essential nonsense. Doodling does lend itself to practical purposes (Figure 9.1), however, because thumbnail sketches are no more complicated than doodles. The only difference is the forethought involved.

The following examples showcase a rogue's gallery of bizarre doodled characters harvested from the deepest recesses of my mind (**FIGURES 3.44-3.54**). I've also included a project walk-through where I show you how I narrowed down a collection of doodles and thumbnail sketches into a rather hairy self-promotional piece (**FIGURES 3.55–3.59**).

FIGURE 3.44 **Meet Mr. Crusty Pants. He loves spinning a good conspiracy yarn.**

FIGURE 3.45 A prophetic look at social media in the year 2018: Aged Twitter acolytes genetically modify themselves with bird DNA, while slinging verbal arrows and smoking government-approved big pharma.

FIGURE 3.46 A watcher.

FIGURE 3.47 Hurry up and formulate your persona.

FIGURE 3.48 Pac-Man has fallen on hard times. He also likes to swear in Klingon.

FIGURE 3.49 Sometimes current events inspire my doodles, like this incarnation of H1N1.

FIGURE 3.51 Dead ideas.

FIGURE 3.52 Stake your claim before the crazies get here.

FIGURE 3.50 Abe's lesser-known brother Willy.

FIGURE 3.53 Harry realizes he has a mold problem.

FIGURE 3.54 "Escape."

FIGURE 3.55 Sometimes the best marketing ideas leverage pop culture. I decided here that I wanted to draw from the hype social media was creating and produce a fun and interactive marketing piece that also served as a self-promotion for my illustration work. These are the thumbnail sketches for my idea, an illustrative mask inspired by Twitter.

FIGURE 3.56 More thumbnail sketches and the isolated direction.

FIGURE 3.57 The refined sketch, ready to scan in.

FIGURE 3.58 No guesswork vector-building using the refined sketch as our guide.

FIGURE 3.59 Final illustrative mask titled, "Twitter Beard," worn by my snarky daughter Savannah.

CHAPTER 4

Getting to the Points

A Bézier curve or path is only as elegant, graceful, or accurate as the anchor points that control and shape it. And in order to better control and edit anchor points, you first need to understand and recognize what qualifies as a good anchor point and path, a bad anchor point and path, and an ugly anchor point and path.

A vector design can easily have hundreds of paths and thousands of anchor points within it. Each point that is incorrectly used or sloppily handled will just add to the overall degradation of your visual aesthetic.

Anyone can learn to use a digital tool; that is merely a skill set. I want you to become a vector craftsperson, someone who can handle the basic tools and create professional results. You may conceive of a brilliant idea, but if your vector craftsmanship is weak, it doesn't matter how well thought out the idea is. It will suffer from poor execution.

On Prime Point Placement

There is one assumption to make before we can determine if an anchor point is good, bad, or ugly. We will assume you have the Prime Point Placement (PPP) of your anchor point correct. That is, you have each anchor point in the correct position within your design. We'll go over placing and removing anchor points, as well as PPP in more detail in the next chapter. But suffice it to say for now that if an anchor point is not positioned correctly as you build your vector shape, it will make controlling the path so that it matches your drawing far more difficult and possibly inaccurate.

For sake of demonstration, all of the vector art in the following images (**FIGURES 4.1–4.3**) contain identical PPP. That is, the anchor points are in the right places. The only difference among the figures will be found in the specific problematic characteristics associated with the individual anchor points.

With that graphic caveat in mind, let's take a closer look.

The Good Anchor Point and Path

In order to demonstrate the good, the bad, and the ugly as those qualities apply to anchor points and paths, I've selected an ornament design that contains only one straight line and depends mainly on the use of Bézier curves to form its shape.

First, however, you must understand the difference between corner anchor points and smooth anchor points. Corner anchor points are placed anywhere your art has an apex that comes to a point. These types of anchor points can be used with or without Bézier curve handles pulled out from one or both sides when the transition between two paths doesn't need to be smooth.

A *smooth* anchor point is placed anywhere your art needs a curve that transitions from one path into the next. This sort of anchor point *always* uses Bézier curve handles pulled out from both sides to control the shape of the Bézier curve.

The following images (**FIGURES 4.1–4.3**) show the anchor points and path build shape on the left and the resulting final shape on the right.

FIGURE 4.1 All of the anchor points in this vector ornament design are of the correct type, either corner or smooth depending on their PPP. The anchor points controlling the Bézier curves that form the main vine in this motif bend smoothly from one side to the other.

The handles are parallel with one another and are not pulled out too far, ensuring a smooth continuity throughout the art. The other anchor point handles that form the remaining Bézier curves are also not overextended, pulled out only as far as needed to form each of the various shapes in the path.

The end result of good anchor points and paths is a graceful and elegant shape.

The Bad Anchor Point and Path

FIGURE 4.2 The anchor points in this vector ornament design are the correct type, but their handles are incorrect. They aren't parallel with one another, so the Bézier curves look less elegant and you begin to lose the visual continuity of the overall path. A consistent creative process that utilizes PPP and The Clockwork Method (which will be covered in chapter 5) will help you steer clear of this problem. At this point, the goal is simply for you to recognize that something is definitely not right. The end result of bad anchor points and paths is a less graceful and more clunky shape.

The Ugly Anchor Point and Path

FIGURE 4.3 Almost all of the anchor points in this vector ornament design are the incorrect type. Any Bézier curve that you want to transition smoothly from one side of an anchor point to the opposite side should always utilize smooth anchor points, not corner anchor points. Using the wrong type of anchor point will cause a curved shape to look pointed.

More problems: Many of the anchor point handles aren't parallel with one another and some are pulled out too far, which prevents a continuous flow through the art and makes parts of it look flat. Some of the other anchor point handles that form the remaining Bézier curves in the design are overextended as well.

Some of these problems emerge from sloppy building and lack of attention to detail, as well as not building vector art point-by-point or shape-building (that is, autotracing). It all comes down to proper craftsmanship.

FIGURE 4.4 This shows the final ornament design. This graphic contains 276 anchor points that make up one path.

A Scrutinizing Eye

Throughout the vector build process, you'll need to pay close attention to your anchor points and paths to ensure you're creating quality. That said, no one is perfect; you'll make mistakes as you create your vector art, so it's important to train yourself to spot potential problems with your anchor points.

It may initially seem like I'm asking you to micro-manage your vector art, and in part that is true. But over time it will become second nature, to the point that you won't even consciously think about which anchor points to place or handles to pull. You will, however, notice the steady improvement of the vector shapes that you'll create because of your due diligence.

The Vector No-Fly List

Be on the look-out for the following common vector building mistakes:

1. **Incorrect Anchor Point:** If you're creating a Bézier curve that bends smoothly from one side of an anchor point to the opposite side as shown in FIGURE 4.5, you need to always use a smooth anchor point rather than a corner anchor point. If a curve looks pointed, then an incorrect anchor point is being used in the Bézier curve.

   To convert a corner anchor point to a smooth anchor point (and vice-versa), just select the problem point and click the "Convert selected anchor points to smooth" button in the Control panel shown in Figure 4.5. The opposite option will appear if the point is already smooth. (Unfortunately, there is no keyboard command for this, nor is it recordable via actions.)

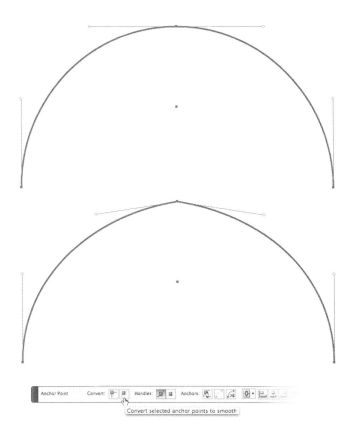

FIGURE 4.5 The correct use of a smooth anchor point shown on top; an incorrect corner anchor point, which causes a pointed look, is shown below.

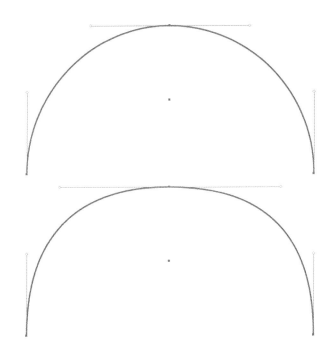

FIGURE 4.6 Properly extended anchor point handles shown on top; a curve with overextended anchor point handles, which cause a flat appearance, is shown below.

2. **Flat Curves:** If you pull out your anchor point handles too far on a Bézier curve that bends smoothly from one side of an anchor point to the opposite side, as shown in FIGURE 4.6, the curve will lose its roundness and begin to look flat. It's a telltale sign of overextended handles.

3. **Parallels:** When you create shapes that contain corresponding Bézier curves that bend smoothly from one side of an anchor point to the opposite side, as shown in FIGURE 4.7, you want to make sure the extended handles at the apex of the path are parallel with one another. If the end vector shape doesn't have a graceful flow, it's a good bet some of the handles aren't parallel.

4. **Overextended Handles:** This is the result of trying to span the distance between two anchor points using one anchor point handle instead of using both. Much like the flat curve problem, it will result in a shape that is flat, awkward, and clunky. But it also can cause mitering problems on severe angles if you decide to add a heavier stroke to your art later (FIGURE 4.8).

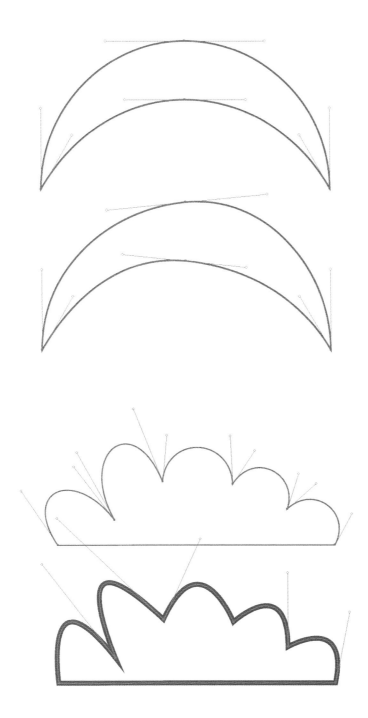

FIGURE 4.7 Parallel handles shown on top; non-parallel handles, which cause an uneven result, are shown below.

FIGURE 4.8 Both handles properly pulled out to form each Bézier curve is shown on top; the use of one overextended handle, which causes flatness, a clunky shape, and mitering problems, is shown below.

A Good Example

It's good to have a critical eye when scrutinizing your vector work as you build to ensure you're avoiding the telltale signs of problematic anchor points and the Bézier curves they control.

But one could argue that it's more important to recognize good anchor point characteristics. As your eye develops, you'll be able to look at any vector graphic and pinpoint either the good or bad characteristics of its anchor points and curves.

FIGURE 4.9 This complex vector ornament design doesn't contain any straight lines. It completely depends on precisely built Bézier curves created from smooth and corner anchor points. You won't find any of this design's content on the "no-fly list."

I should point out that the design shown in **FIGURES 4.9** and **4.10** took me about eight hours to build. I had to rebuild several shapes a few times before I dialed in the vector art precisely. I mention this because it would be easy for me to say that if you follow my process, everything will be easy and work the first time. That isn't true.

FIGURE 4.10 Final vector artwork I created for a die-hard Mac fanboy who loves his Apple iPad so much that he hired me to design this custom ornament, which he'll have etched onto the back of it.

FIELD NOTES

Change Your Perspective

When scrutinizing your vector shapes, it's a good idea to select and rotate or flip them, print them out larger, or change your view to outline in Adobe Illustrator in order to pinpoint problem areas you can improve on. If you don't do this, it's too easy for your eyes to get used to what they are looking at.

Changing the visual perspective and orientation of the art forces the mind to reassess the shapes in your design and determine if something needs to be fixed. It's the same principle as holding a drawing up to a mirror in order to discover a distortion.

We'll talk more about self-art direction in Chapter 8.

What is true about my process is that it is a *process*. Part of that process is recognizing the good and bad characteristics in your own art and in the art of others. While creating this design I had to remind myself of The Clockwork Method (or TCM, a very handy method we'll introduce in Chapter 5). I wasn't following it, and my shapes were looking wonky.

Thank God for Command\Control-Z

Even using this systematic approach for building vector graphics, not every piece of vector artwork you create will be perfect. I still make mistakes every day. Placing anchor points and manipulating handles takes some trial and error.

The ultimate goal of this book is to dramatically reduce your potential for making vector mistakes, help you to recognize when something isn't right , and show you how to fix problems quickly so you can continue building your designs. So when in doubt, Command-Z (or Control-Z) can be your best form of creative accountability.

DESIGN DRILLS:
Vector Skeletons

Proper anchor point placement is critical for creating precise vector artwork. But, unless you have your vector paths selected (V), it can be difficult to tell where all of the anchor points reside within a given design.

On the next four pages, we'll take a closer look at the vector skeletons within two very different sorts of design projects so you can see exactly where all of the anchor points are placed and how those placements affect the final results.

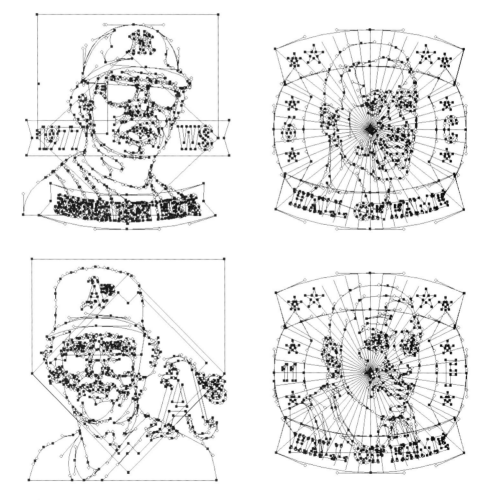

FIGURE 4.11 When you view the sketelal points and paths of these patch designs, created for Major League Baseball (MLB) and National Basketball Association (NBA) licensed products, they reveal that some of the vector content is masked. You can't see it in the final art shown in Figure 4.12.

FIGURE 4.12 The final official MLB- and NBA-licensed patch designs.

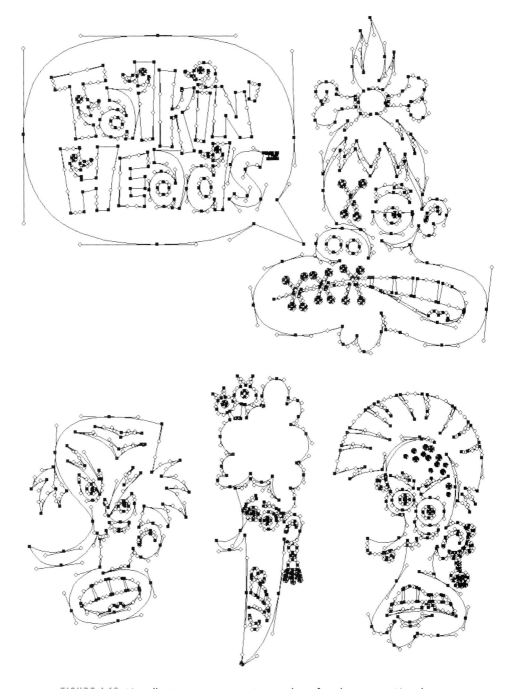

FIGURE 4.13 Not all art requires a massive number of anchor points. Note how I only needed seven anchor points to form the speech bubble in this logotype design for a custom art product.

FIGURE 4.14 This final art shows only four of the 50 "talkin' heads" I created for the company Veer.

CHAPTER 5

Shape Surveillance

It's time to take your refined drawing out of analog and move it into the digital realm. In order to do this accurately, you must know exactly where to place your anchor points in order to precisely form the paths needed to create your final vector shapes.

It does no good to spend time up front drawing and refining the shapes in your art on paper only to fall short by building them poorly on screen. Placing points incorrectly wastes time in the build stage of your creative process, and ultimately, you end up with imprecise vector results.

I can't stress enough the importance of proper anchor point placement. You must be able to look at any visual shape, drawn or otherwise, and know exactly how you'd go about building it, anchor point by anchor point. This chapter will show you how to start the build process; chapter 6 will show you how to finish the build accurately.

The Clockwork Method

The simpler the shape, the easier it is to discern where to place anchor points. When the shapes that make up your art get more complex, however, it can get trickier.

To help you in your shape study, I've created "The Clockwork Method" (TCM). It's a simple way to look at any shape and then know precisely where to place points. Basically, you imagine the clock face in your mind, rotate it as needed to orient with the shapes in your art, and use it as a guide.

When you initially learned how to use a drawing program like Adobe Illustrator, more than likely no one taught you where to place your anchor points when building your vector shapes. Most often the focus is solely on the tools that you use to create vector graphics and not on the creative process that utilizes the tools.

Over time and through trial and error, many are able to develop their skills enough to make it work for their needs. Most still struggle, though, to pull off well-crafted vector shapes. The source of that struggle can be blamed on not knowing exactly where to place the anchor points that make up the design you wish to create.

I know this was true for me. And it was only when I started teaching advanced digital illustration at a local college that I developed a coherent method that I could relate to my students and demystify the process of anchor point placement. The Clockwork Method circumvents all of the hassles of figuring everything out piecemeal over a period of years.

A circle provides the simplest illustration of TCM. The circle would receive anchor points at the 12-, 3-, 6-, and 9-o'clock positions (FIGURE 5.1). More complex shapes that contain both concave and convex curves won't necessarily receive all four points every time, but we'll talk about that more in a bit.

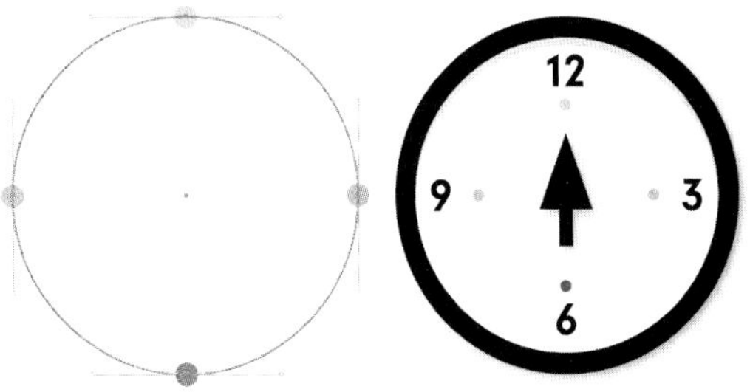

For shapes that are not straight up-and-down, you can also tilt the clock face so that it better corresponds with that shape. FIGURE 5.2 shows not only how the tilt works, but how it easily adapts to the situation and your preference in regard to anchor point placement. The 9 o'clock anchor point (highlighted blue on the left) could just as well be discerned by someone else as a 12 o'clock (highlighted green on the right) by rotating the clock in his or her mind 90 degrees instead. The Prime Point Placement, or PPP, on both is still correct using TCM. (More on PPP in a bit.) It all depends on how you see it in your mind.

FIGURE 5.1 A vector circle shape is shown at left; note how it corresponds to the clock positions on the right. I've used four different colors on the TCM clock as well as on the circle art so that you can see the correspondence here and in upcoming illustrations.

FIGURE 5.2 In this example, the 12-o'clock position is shown in two different orientations. Both are correct. Every person sees the clock orientation in his or her mind differently, but the end result is that both orientations match the curves in the art.

As Figure 5.2 suggests, your art is bound to contain many shapes, perhaps hundreds. Each individual curve that makes up the overall shape of your art will have its own custom-angled clock face.

It's just that simple and just that flexible. From now on, I want you to look at every shape you need to build in vector form through the transparent clock face of TCM. It will help remove the guesswork when you place your anchor points.

Train Your Brain

I realize this method may feel a bit strange at first, but using TCM is nothing more than a mental trick to help you look at any form, isolate the various shapes (or curves) that are in it, and associate them with a clock orientation in your mind to discern the anchor point placements.

Let's start by isolating shapes. In FIGURE 5.3 and FIGURE 5.4, you can see how I isolate particular areas of my art. Some curves define interior shapes, while some define exterior shapes. Once my visual associations with these shapes are identified using TCM, I can now properly discern my placement of the anchor points as shown in Figure 5.4.

FIGURE 5.5 provides a more challenging design for your TCM consideration. The shapes are freeform and might mentally require us to rotate and orient our clock to match its curves.

As we did in Figures 5.3 and 5.4, we'll begin to associate our mental clock with the shapes in our drawn form. Remember that when you make these visual associations, you may not use all four points on the clock to form the needed shape. If you look at Figure 5.4, you'll notice many of the anchor point placements on the left side only required one point association with the clock to form the needed curve.

FIGURE 5.6 shows how I see the first clock orientation in my mind. As demonstrated in Figures 5.3 and 5.4, I want you to continue the shape surveillance by studying the drawn art and using TCM to discern where the anchor points would be placed according to the clock in your own mind. Compare with FIGURE 5.7 and see how well you did.

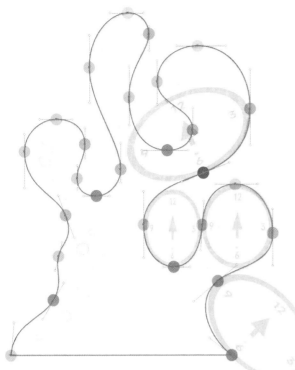

FIGURE 5.3 The illustration shows how I discerned the shapes in my art using TCM. This is a step that I imagine only in my mind. The faded clocks demonstrate how I orient the faces in my mind before placing my anchor points.

FIGURE 5.4 I continue to use TCM to discern all of my anchor point placements and precisely form the path shape needed to match my drawing.

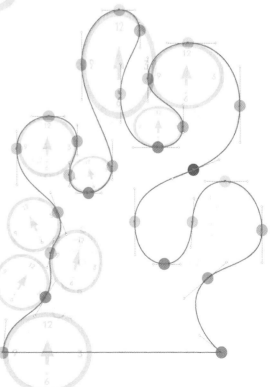

FIGURE 5.5 Look at this drawn shape and discern where you'd place anchor points using TCM. You may not need to use all four clock points on every curved shape.

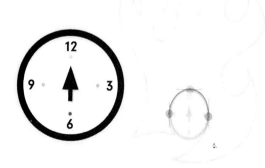

FIGURE 5.6 Using TCM, I've discerned the first shape in the form. Can you discern the rest? Refer to Figures 5.3 and 5.4 for help if you need it.

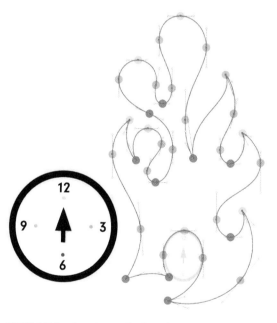

FIGURE 5.7 This shows all of the final TCM locations of the anchor points. How did your discernment compare to this?

You'll build your vector art one anchor point at a time, mentally picturing the clock, rotating it if needed, and associating the point on the clock with the anchor point you need to place to form the specific curve within the drawn form. Some curved shapes may associate with one or more points of the clock; it all depends on how you visualize it in your mind. Once you've discerned an anchor point's location, you place it and then move to the next shape in your design and repeat the same process until you have the entire vector path built as shown in **FIGURE 5.8**.

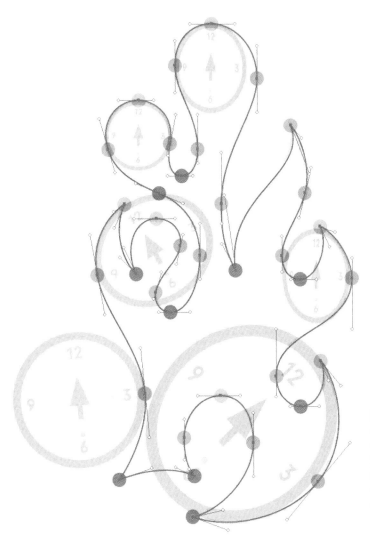

FIGURE 5.8 **This shows many of the mental TCM discernments we made as we built the vector path in order to determine the final Prime Point Placement (or PPP), which we'll cover in greater detail later in this chapter).**

Applying The Clockwork Method

Of course, all shapes aren't as simple as the circle shown in Figure 5.1. And, naturally, art usually contains many shapes and curves with many different angles. Still, discerning the anchor point placement on any shape is easier if you use TCM. Regardless of how irregular a shape may be, if you think of it as a clock, you'll be able to place the anchor points with greater accuracy.

Let's try TCM on a more complex shape. Remember, the first step is to analyze the shapes in the art (**FIGURE 5.9**). Then, think of the clock positions and how they can be roughly approximated on those shapes. (Again, refer to Figures 5.3 and 5.4.) Because of the angles in the shapes of this flame motif, we'll rotate our mental clock to associate it with the many curves within the art.

Where do you start? The most obvious anchor point placements within any design are the areas that come to a point. Those are no-brainers, and it's a good place to start your building because you don't have to discern anything. These are absolutes: Any area of your art that comes to a point gets a point (**FIGURE 5.10**).

After you've identified all of the angles that come to a point, you can move on to determine the other coordinates (**FIGURES 5.10–5.13**).

The more you train your brain to discern shapes using TCM, the easier it gets. Like anything new, it feels awkward and strange at first, but stick with it and you'll enjoy the results.

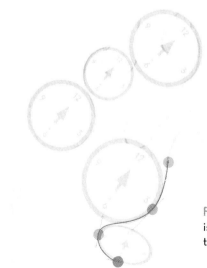

FIGURE 5.9 **The first step is to perform shape surveillance by isolating the various curved shapes and mentally associating them with a clock.**

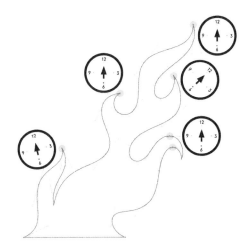

FIGURE 5.10 Most of the points in this design are corner anchor points since most of the shapes come to a point. The rest of the points associate with a mental clock orientation of 12 o'clock.

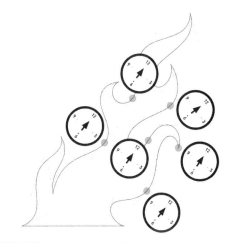

FIGURE 5.11 Here are all of the anchor points in this flame motif that match my mental clock orientation of 3 o'clock.

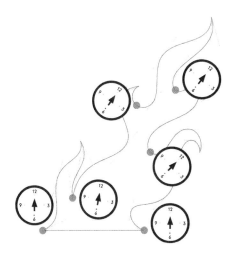

FIGURE 5.12 Here are all of the anchor points that match my mental clock orientation of 6 o'clock.

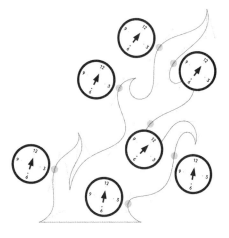

FIGURE 5.13 Here are all of the anchor points that match my mental clock orientation of 9 o'clock.

There are many variables that will affect the quality of your vector art, as we discussed in chapters 3 and 4. But the most important fundamental aspect of building your vector graphics starts with your anchor point locations. Get the anchor point locations wrong, and you'll have a hard time building.

We'll get into this in more detail a little later in this chapter when we discuss Prime Point Placement (PPP) later in this chapter.

More on Rotating Your Clock

As I mentioned before, when a shape within your design is angled, it helps to also angle your clock face to match it. Since this can be more confusing than a simple north/south orientation, let's consider another example.

If you look at FIGURE 5.14, you'll notice that many of the anchor points run along paths that are angled. In such cases, simply set your mental clock face to the same angle and start placing points. This is an instance for which one clock face can accommodate all of the angles. (I should point out that you could also select the vector art and your placed refined sketch and rotate them to align with a normal north/south TCM orientation. I've done that on occasion, but it isn't always practical.)

FIGURE 5.14 If a shape demands a path that needs an anchor point that falls outside the normal orientation of TCM, just rotate the TCM clock to match the angle of your shape.

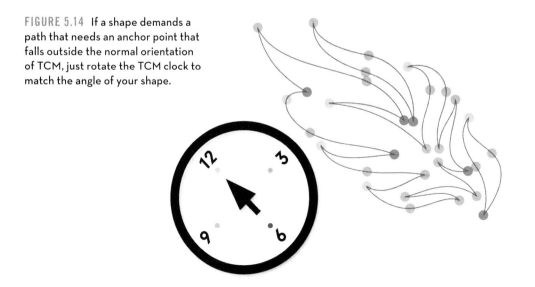

Most designs that you'll build will require using both the normal (north/south) orientation and a wide variety of rotated TCM orientations, like the example in the next section.

Building Complex Shapes

To demonstrate TCM on an even more complex shape, let's look at the elegant ornament design in FIGURE 5.15. The shapes in this art demand precise Bézier curves that can only be achieved if the anchor points are in the correct locations.

As always, TCM is the key to success (FIGURES 5.16–5.19).

FIGURE 5.15 Using TCM, I'll begin to perform shape surveillance on my refined sketch to figure out where to place my initial anchor points. The obvious locations are the corner anchor points found at each end of the vines. If your shape has a point, it'll get a point.

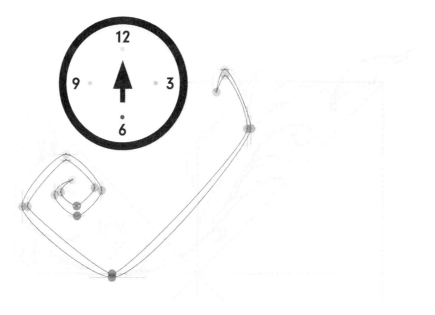

FIGURE 5.16 Using my refined sketch as my road map, I place my initial anchor points using TCM. At this stage, the correspondence of the drawn lines to the sketch lines underneath is not perfect. But it is the effective placement of the points that will ultimately create handles in just the right spots for pushing and pulling things into shape.

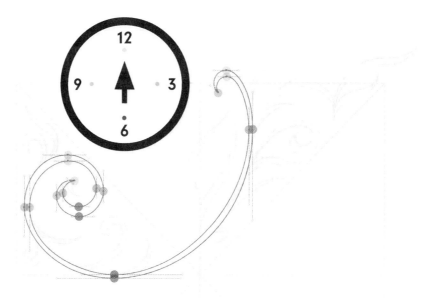

FIGURE 5.17 Once my anchor points are located in their correct positions, it's simply a matter of pulling out my Bézier curve handles to shape the path so it matches my refined drawing.

FIGURE 5.18 I continue to utilize TCM to build all of the individual shapes that make up this ornament design (points and handles are hidden here). I'm using both normal and rotated TCM orientations to pull off all of my shapes. (We'll cover shape building in greater detail in chapter 6.)

FIGURE 5.19 The final vector artwork for the ornament design.

Prime Point Placement

At the risk of sounding redundant, not to mention redundant, this bears repeating: When it comes to building your design using vector methods, it's of paramount importance that the initial anchor points you place are in the best possible locations as they relate to the shape you're attempting to form.

The paths in your final vector shape and the Bézier curves they utilize will be only as precise as the anchor points that control them. You want to make sure that the Prime Point Placement (PPP) of your anchor points is correct.

TCM will get you in the right neighborhood, but PPP will pinpoint the exact address at which your anchor point will live. Determining the exact location is a process, not an event, so you'll be leveraging both methods to fine-tune point locations.

Making a Point!

In chapter 4, we discovered there are only two types of anchor points, corner and smooth. Knowing how each controls a Bézier curve and path will help us understand where to place them using TCM and PPP.

1. **Corner Anchor Point:** You'll place a corner anchor point anywhere your art has an apex that comes to a point. These types of anchor points can be used with or without Bézier curve handles pulled out from one or both sides when the transition between two paths doesn't need to be smooth (FIGURE 5.20).

2. **Smooth Anchor Point:** You'll place a smooth anchor point anywhere your art needs a curve that transitions from one path into the next. This sort of anchor point *always* uses Bézier curve handles pulled out from both sides to control the shape of the curve (FIGURE 5.21).

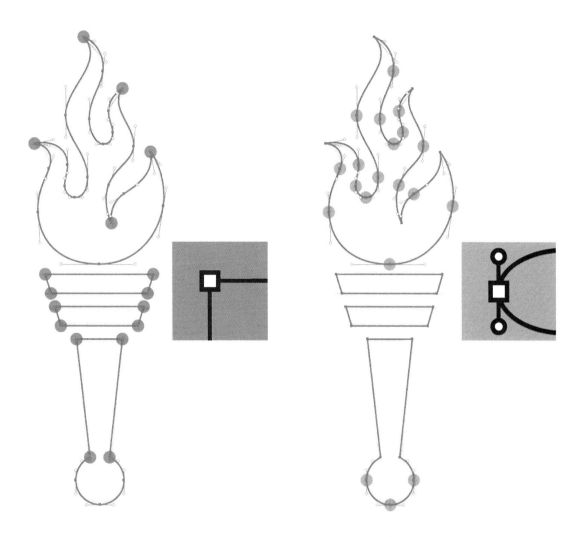

FIGURE 5.20 There are a total of 17 corner anchor points within the build shapes of this torch graphic (highlighted in orange). The handle shapes are made mostly from corner anchor points.

FIGURE 5.21 There are a total of 20 smooth anchor points within the build shapes of this torch graphic (highlighted in purple). The flame contains numerous Bézier curves, so most of the anchor points to shape it are smooth.

Combining PPP and TCM

Let's take a closer look at a more complex vector graphic. Like before, we'll study the refined sketch and consider how to place our anchor points initially using TCM and then we'll use PPP to build the art precisely (FIGURES 5.22–5.25).

Note that the final design for this example (shown in FIGURE 5.25) is symmetrical, so we only have to build half of it—we'll copy the final paths and flip them to form our final art. (We'll cover more benefits of symmetrical design in the next chapter.)

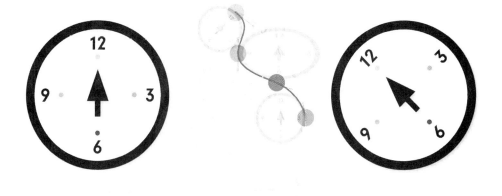

FIGURE 5.22 Using TCM, I begin to perform shape surveillance on my refined sketch, discerning my anchor point placement and orienting my clock to associate with the shapes, rotating it as needed.

FIGURE 5.23 All of the anchor points in this vector ornament design are the correct type, either corner or smooth, depending on their PPP. Corner anchor points are highlighted in orange.

FIGURE 5.24 The smooth anchor points that control the Bézier curves, which bend smoothly from one side of the anchor point to the other, are highlighted in purple.

FIGURE 5.25 The final vector artwork for the ornament design was created by copying and flipping the paths created in the previous steps.

The Yin and Yang of Anchor Points

Don't assume you'll get your TCM correct all the time. No one is perfect. And when collaborating with others, you'll eventually be able to spot problem areas in their work as well. These are the most common problems:

1. **Wrong Anchor Point:** Make sure you are using the correct type of anchor point in your path, either corner or smooth.

2. **PPP Isn't Correct:** Some of your anchor points are still not in their correct positions to enable you to control the Bézier curves accurately. Go through your path and review each anchor point with TCM in mind and double check the PPP for each.

3. **Not Enough Anchor Points in Path:** You haven't placed enough anchor points to form the shape accurately. You are likely struggling to form the exact Bézier curves needed to make the path shape. Review your shape with TCM in mind and add anchor points on your path where needed using the Add Anchor Point Tool (+) (**FIGURE 5.26**).

4. **Too Many Anchor Points in Path:** You've placed too many anchor points to form the shape with precision. It will be hard to control the path shape and retain an elegant form. Review your shape with TCM in mind and remove the unnecessary anchor points from your path using the Delete Anchor Point Tool (–) (**FIGURE 5.27**). A well-built vector shape should contain only the amount of anchor points needed to pull it off. No more, no less.

FIGURE 5.26 Not enough anchor points have been placed to build the shape correctly. A telltale sign is overextended Bézier handles.

FIGURE 5.27   Too many anchor points have been placed here, which ruins the graceful shape of the design. Managing all of the small Bézier curve handles makes shaping curves a major pain in the keester.

An example: The anchor points in the design shown in Figure 5.26 are actually in their correct PPP, but the path doesn't contain enough placed anchor points to build the shape precisely. A telltale sign you're not using enough anchor points is overextended Bézier curve handles.

Trying to build precise vector paths with overextended Bézier handles is like trying to paint a picture using a six-foot-long brush. You couldn't stand close enough to your canvas to control your forms, and clearly the art would pay the price. The same is true with overextended Bézier handles. If you can't control your forms with precision, your design will wind up paying the price.

Many of the anchor points in the design shown in Figure 5.27 are in their correct PPP, but the path contains far too many anchor points to form the shape gracefully. It ends up looking clunky.

FIGURE 5.28 All anchor points are in their correct PPP, and the shape contains
the correct balance of anchor points needed to create the final shape accurately.
The end result is a more elegant form.

An unnecessary anchor point by definition can never be in a correct
PPP. Delete the points from your path and simplify the shape.

Your ultimate goal is balance (**FIGURE 5.28**). After placing the anchor
points and shaping the Bézier curves with their handles to form your art,
you'll know immediately if you haven't placed enough or if you've placed
too many to build it accurately. Be diligent in your surveillance, and you'll
see massive improvements in your design.

The more you utilize TCM, the more you'll avoid these common vector
pitfalls. It's important that you're able to recognize problematic attributes in your own design and the design of others you work with so you
can improve the quality and consistently create at a higher level.

Deconstructing the Vector Monster

Feeling overwhelmed? Let's deconstruct a a real-world project with TCM and PPP in mind. Then you will be ready for learning the various build methods presented in chapter 6.

I created this illustration for a publishing company. Using TCM and PPP to build core shapes played a key role in building the final vector artwork.

Of course, smart vector build methods were also crucial in this project's success. We'll be vetting them more fully in the next chapter. That said, it's kind of like love and marriage: you can't have one without the other. That's why it's important to see everything in context, as we will here.

1. **The Clockwork Method:** First, I performed shape surveillance and analyzed the shapes in my refined sketch using TCM as shown in **FIGURE 5.29**.

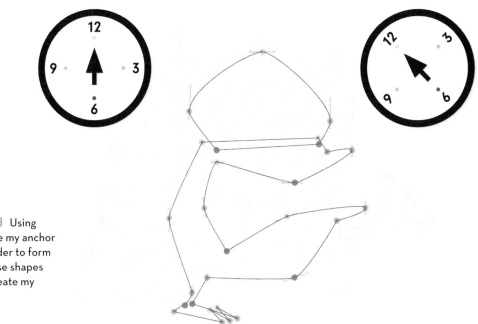

FIGURE 5.29 Using TCM, I place my anchor points in order to form the core base shapes I need to create my artwork.

2. **Prime Point Placement:** At this point, I may zoom in on my anchor points and move them into more precise locations to facilitate accurate Bézier curves, as shown in **FIGURE 5.30**.

3. **Vector Build Methods:** I continue to build every vector shape needed to create my final art using TCM, PPP, and additional vector build methods that we'll go over in chapter 6 (**FIGURES 5.31** and **5.32**).

4. **Final Artwork:** Once all of my core shapes are built, I move on to coloring my vector art. Once coloring is done, I'll continue to use TCM, PPP, and additional vector build methods that we'll cover in the next chapter to build the various shapes needed for detailing my final artwork (**FIGURE 5.33**).

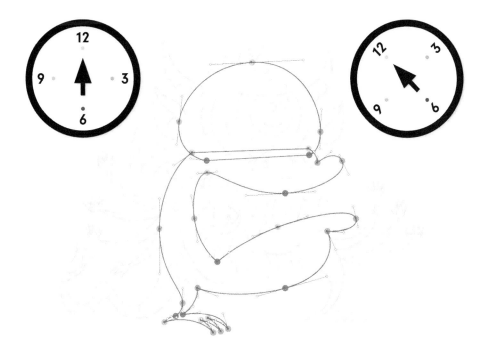

FIGURE 5.30 With my PPP locked in, I pull out my Bézier curve handles and complete the shaping of my core base shapes.

FIGURE 5.31 I build every vector shape I can using the "Point by Point" method (which we'll cover in the next chapter).

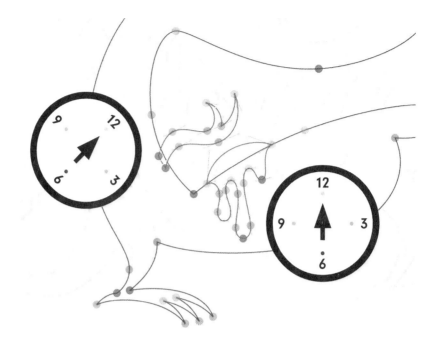

FIGURE 5.32 All the vector shapes needed to create my final art are now built using TCM, PPP, and additional build methods that we'll cover in chapter 6.

FIGURE 5.33 The final monster vector illustration.
His name is "Blinky."

When you're out in the public, take notice of the various shapes that are around you. Maybe it's a shadow on someone's shirt, the profile of a face, or the shape of a bush. Once you've noticed a shape, ask yourself the following questions regarding how you'd build it in vector form:

• Where would you place the points using TCM?

• What types of points would you need to use?

• What areas of the shape would need Bézier curves?

• How many individual shapes would make up the final form needed?

Creative habits like this may be unorthodox, but I guarantee they will help improve your shape discernment.

Progressive Improvements

Building your vector shapes using the systematic creative process I describe can seem like a monstrous task even for a simple design. To manage a complex design that can easily contain thousands of points and hundreds of paths might seem impossible. But with practice and time, it gets easier and the process becomes second nature.

You'll never get your PPP absolutely correct the first time all the time. But the more you get into the habit of using TCM, the more consistently your anchor points will fall within the correct vector zip code as you build.

TCM and PPP are actually the first steps in the "Point by Point" build method that we'll introduce in chapter 6. This process will help you even more. And in chapter 8, you'll learn how to art direct yourself, an invaluable creative and managerial tool.

DESIGN DRILLS:
Spotting Clocks

When you get in the habit of using The Clockwork Method (TCM) to build your vector art, you'll start to see clocks in every vector-based design you look at, whether you designed it or not. And that's a good thing.

To kick-start the habit, let's take a look at a handful of designs from my portfolio and see where the clocks show up.

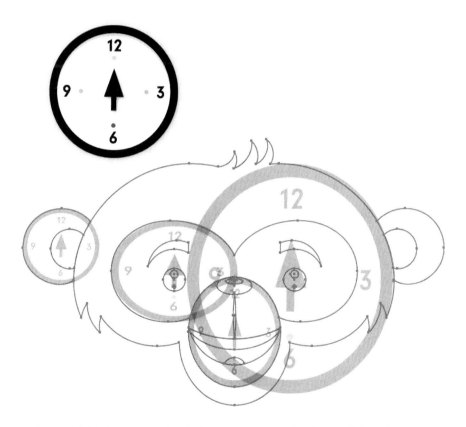

FIGURE 5.34 Sometimes the clock you associate with a shape will form the entire shape, and sometimes it will just help create part of the shape.

FIGURE 5.35 This chimptastic monkey character illustration was
for a kid's play area in Utah.

FIGURE 5.36 Here, I apply TCM to guide me as I build letterforms in a logotype design.

FIGURE 5.37 Logotype design concept for new line of Pepsi drinks.

FIGURE 5.38 Remember, this is a mental trick to help you discern your anchor point placements. Polly want a clock?

FIGURE 5.39 This package illustration concept for ZuPreem, an exotic pet food line, was loved by the agency and client, but ultimately it failed in test marketing.

CHAPTER 6

Vector Build Methods

As you approach a design that needs to be built in vector form, you must have your rules of creative engagement thoroughly defined. This means knowing what specific type of build method will work best for your design so that your final art will be both precise and professional.

In chapter 5, we covered two shape surveillance techniques: The Clockwork Method (TCM) and Prime Point Placement (PPP). In this chapter, we'll leverage both techniques as we build art using another technique I have developed: the point-by-point method. As mentioned in chapter 5, TCM gets your points in the right neighborhood, and PPP gets them to the right address. The point-by-point method builds the actual structure.

In this chapter, you'll also learn another construction technique: the shape-building method. The shape-building method does just what it advertises: It builds shapes (with points conveniently already in place) using familiar Illustrator tools.

For the majority of the vector artwork that you'll build, you'll need to use both the point-by-point method and the shape-building method. They work together like an artistic tag team in building vector shapes. How do you know when to use which method? It depends on the shape that you need to create.

- You'll use the point-by-point method to create any shapes that are free-flowing and organic. Any form that has a lot of curvature to it that requires complex Bézier curves will utilize this method (FIGURE 6.1).

- You'll use the shape-building method to create any shapes that are more geometric or iconic in nature. Simple forms that can be built using 90-degree angles or that contain circular or square shapes are ideal for the shape-building method (FIGURE 6.2).

  By the way, when you're drawing out your concepts and your design requires a circular shape, or another type of basic geometric form, don't worry about getting it perfect in your refined sketch. You can use the shape-building method to get that job done quickly later on.

Before you begin to build in vector form, do your best to determine what parts will require a point-by-point method and what parts will require the shape-building method in order to create them. The more you utilize both of these build methods to create your vector art, the easier it will be to determine which one to use.

Like wine, your ability to discern what method to use and when to use it improves with age.

FIGURE 6.1 This design was almost entirely built using the point-by-point method. Only the bottom circular shapes utilized the shape-building method.

FIGURE 6.2 This icon set relies heavily upon the shape-building method to create all of the iconic forms shown. Only a few elements required the point-by-point method.

Point-by-Point Method

In chapter 4, I focused on the good, the bad, and the ugly attributes of anchor points, and in chapter 5, we thoroughly defined how to discern where to place anchor points.

The point-by-point method that I'm introducing in this chapter takes the rough forms you created with TCM and PPP and transforms them into polished final art. Here's how it works.

One Point at a Time

When it comes to vector building, there is nothing more fundamental than building your shapes one anchor point at a time—hence, the name "point-by-point." It defines the modus operandi that most people use when working with vectors. I've created a four-step method that will help you optimize the process. The four steps are:

1. **Rough Build:** Using TCM and PPP (see chapter 5), you'll place your anchor points in their correct locations to roughly form the shape you want to build (**FIGURE 6.3**). If an anchor point needs to be smooth, pull the Bézier handles out just enough so you can easily grab them later (in step 4). Don't try to refine the shape too much now; all you want to focus on is the correct anchor point placement.

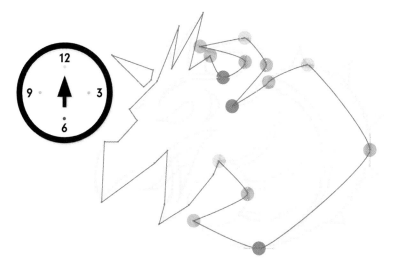

FIGURE 6.3 **Place your anchor points using TCM and PPP as discussed in chapter 5.**

2. **Shape with Xtream Path:** With your anchor points and their corresponding paths in place, you'll now use the Segment Direct Edit tool, which is part of the Xtream Path plug-in (covered in chapter 2). Simply grab anywhere on the path (between any two anchor points) and push or pull it to form the desired shape (**FIGURE 6.4**), adjusting the Bézier curves as needed to match the vector path with the underlying drawing (**FIGURE 6.5**). Don't worry about breaking your smooth anchor points; we'll fix those in the next step and dial it in even more.

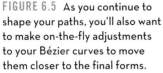

FIGURE 6.4 Form all segments of your path with the Xtream Path plug-in's Segment Direct Edit tool (circled in green) simply by grabbing anywhere on the path and pushing or pulling it into shape. Easy peasy.

FIGURE 6.5 As you continue to shape your paths, you'll also want to make on-the-fly adjustments to your Bézier curves to move them closer to the final forms.

3. **Smooth Anchor Points:** Now, using the Direct Selection tool, select all of the anchor points in your design that should be smooth—*not* corner points (FIGURE 6.6). Once you have them all selected, from the Control panel, using the right-most button of the Convert option, click "Convert selected anchor points to smooth" (FIGURE 6.7). At this point, your vector art is ready to refine. (For more information about anchor points, see chapter 4.)

FIGURE 6.6 All of the anchor points that need to be smooth are selected (circled here in green).

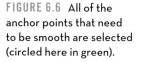
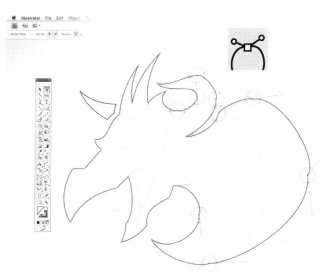

FIGURE 6.7 All selected anchor points are smooth after "Convert selected anchor points to smooth" is clicked in the Control panel (circled here in orange).

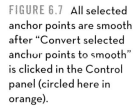
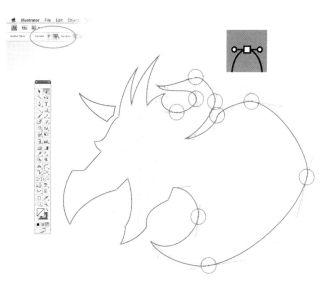

4. **Refine Shapes:** It's time to focus more closely on the Bézier curves and pull their handles out to refine the path shape. Notice in FIGURE 6.8 how the Bézier handles are parallel where necessary to ensure precise curves. You'll also want to re-scrutinize your anchor point locations and make any small PPP corrections necessary in order to form an accurate vector shape. (Review Prime Point Placement in chapter 5.)

FIGURE 6.8 Take your time and pay attention to the PPP and your Bézier curve handles to ensure that they aren't overextended. Be sure to shape the paths elegantly to match your drawing precisely.

FIGURE 6.9 Continue to build the remaining vector shapes needed to produce your final art. (Note: Some of the new shapes, such as the arches that cut into the front of and define the back of the character's neck, were created using the shape-building method that we'll cover later in this chapter.)

FIGURE 6.10 This shows the final vector artwork and several other avatar designs I created for an RPG game. My vector building utilized TCM, PPP, and the point-by-point method, plus the shape-building method (described later in this chapter).

At first, these four steps might seem laborious if you're not used to building your vector artwork this way, but over time all of the methods that I cover in this book will become second nature to you. Once you get used to them, you won't consciously have to think about each step of the process. It will all just be part of your natural workflow. Use these methods consistently in your work, and you'll soon see your vector build times lessen and your level of precision increase.

So no whining: Stay consistent and expect to struggle through this until it becomes your new normal. You won't be sorry.

FIGURE 6.11 To form the Bézier curve elegantly and with precise control, I used three anchor points to shape this ornament accurately.

Span the Distance Wisely

When you create any Bézier curve in your design, you'll need to analyze the length of that curved path and determine how many anchor points you'll need to form it precisely.

Getting your anchor points right is a balance between using just enough to get the job done accurately and not adding too many, which makes it harder to control the form of the vector path. We discussed this tangentially in chapters 4 and 5, but since it's a core aspect of the point-by-point method, we need to focus on it more specifically now. In FIGURES 6.11–6.13, I show how to find the balance between too many and not enough anchor points. Keep TCM and PPP in mind.

FIGURE 6.12 It's technically correct to form the same Bézier curve using only two points, but aesthetically it would be wrong because it just doesn't reproduce the artwork the way I initially drew it. This level of detail is what separates the pros from the amateurs. A pro will take the time to refine the shape, whereas an amateur will usually say, "This is good enough."

FIGURE 6.13 Final vector artwork for this ornament design.

Shape-Building Method

The shape-building method that I describe in this section is ideal for creating geometric shapes. Creating your artwork with one continuous path, point-by-point, isn't always practical, nor is it an efficient use of your time.

This is where the shape-building method comes in. It's a simple and fast way to build precise shapes using one or all of the following tools in Adobe Illustrator: the Rectangle tool (M), the Ellipse tool (L), and the Pathfinder panel (Shift-Command-F9 or Shift-Control-F9). It's faster to build simplified geometric shapes using the shape tools because they will form the entire shape needed with all of the anchor points in place automatically. So it takes less time and will be more precise than manually trying to position each anchor point on a path and then adjusting multiple Bézier curves.

To demonstrate the shape-building method, we'll create a palm leaf in three easy steps.

1. **Basic Vector Shapes:** Using the refined sketch as our guide, choose Rectangle > Tools > Ellipse (L) and create six circle shapes that match the contour of the refined sketch shown in FIGURE 6.14. (See chapter 2 for more information about this tool.)

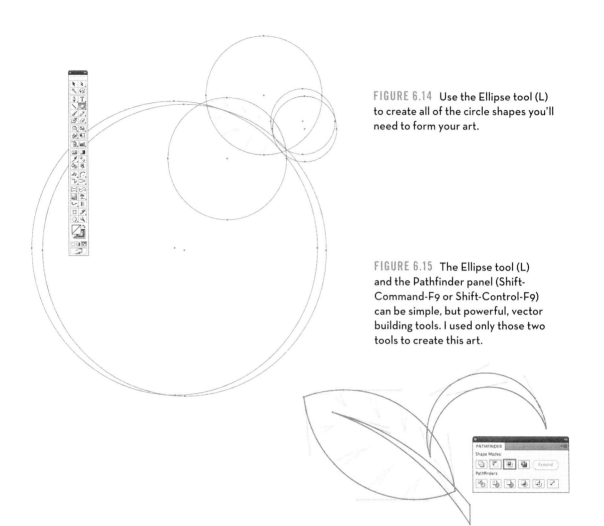

FIGURE 6.14 Use the Ellipse tool (L) to create all of the circle shapes you'll need to form your art.

FIGURE 6.15 The Ellipse tool (L) and the Pathfinder panel (Shift-Command-F9 or Shift-Control-F9) can be simple, but powerful, vector building tools. I used only those two tools to create this art.

2. **Pathfinder Panel** (Shift-Command-F9 or Shift-Control-F9): Select the two circles that make up the shape of the palm leaf design and click the Intersect button in the Pathfinder panel (highlighted in red in FIGURE 6.15). This will create a new shape that is formed by the area where the two original circles overlap. To form the other four circular shapes that make up the stem and the notches of the leaf, select any two shapes and click the Minus Front button (highlighted in green) in the Pathfinder panel to form the shapes you'll need to punch out of the base shape (Figure 6.15). (See chapter 2 for more information on Pathfinder functions.)

3. **Final Shape Building:** Once you have all the necessary shape assets in place (stem and notch shapes) to form your final art, as shown in FIGURE 6.16A, you'll select them all (V-Shift) and then click the Unite button (highlighted in red) within the Pathfinder panel (Shift-Command-F9 or Shift-Control-F9) to form one compound path (FIGURES 6.16B–6.17).

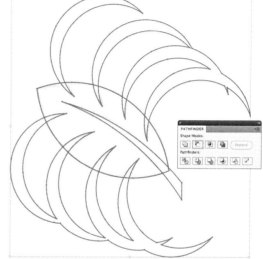

FIGURE 6.16A Select one of the notch shapes on the outside of the leaf. Next, copy (Command-C / Control-C), paste (Command-V / Control-V), and rotate (R) the notch shape seven more times to use the shape for all of the other locations in the palm leaf. (Watch the "Shape-Building Method" video on the DVD.)

FIGURE 6.16B I select the new compound shape and the base palm shape (V-Shift) and click the Minus Front button (highlighted in green) within the Pathfinder panel (Shift-Command-F9 or Shift-Control-F9) to form the final art shape (as shown in Figure 6.17).

FIGURE 6.17 The final vector shape of the palm leaf, which was created using the shape-building method.

FIGURE 6.18 **Final vector art in context.**

The palm leaf is just part of the overall design shown in FIGURE 6.18. The majority of the design relied heavily on the use of the point-by-point building method, but when I got to the palm leaves it made more sense to use the shape-building method instead.

When to Use Which Method

Knowing when to use the shape-building method or the point-by-point method depends on the type of shape you're trying to create. Rarely, if ever, will you build your entire project using one or the other. For the majority of your projects, you'll start building your vector art via the point-by-point method, and sometime during that build process, you'll get to a specific part of your design that will lend itself to the shape-building method.

It's all about discerning the shape you need to build at any given moment and realizing that in one case it would be far easier and more precise to create a certain shape using the shape tools, and in another case it would be better to manually place anchor points and adjust Bézier curves. Let's take a look at a design that requires both methods (FIGURES 6.19–6.24).

FIGURE 6.19 I'll use this refined sketch of a character design as my guide for building vector shapes inside my drawing program.

FIGURE 6.20 Because I took the time to draw out my shapes, I know how to build them, which eliminates guesswork. I use point-by-point building to create the eyebrow and the Ellipse tool (L) to create the circular shapes that make up the eye. I use point-by-point to build the shapes that create the eyebrow because it's more organic and freeform and cannot be built using any of the shape tools. To create the circular shapes that make up the character's eyes, I use the Ellipse tool (L) because the eyes are simple geometric shapes that would be harder to build manually, one anchor point at a time. These are the types of simple build decisions you'll make on the fly as you create your vector forms in Illustrator.

FIGURE 6.21 I continue to use the Ellipse tool (L) to create all of the circular shapes needed to form the contour of the character's arm and hand. The shapes that make up the arm and hand are more geometric than organic, so they naturally lend themselves to using the shape tools instead of manually positioning the anchor points one a time. Using the same methods as we did to create the palm leaf (Figures 6.14–6.17), I select two circular shapes at a time and click the Minus Front button (highlighted in green) within the Pathfinder panel (Shift-Command-F9 or Shift-Control-F9) to create the final arm and hand shown in Figure 6.22.

FIGURE 6.22 The final shape building results.

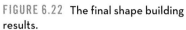

FIGURE 6.23 As I create all of my vector art, I continue to use TCM and PPP (covered in chapter 5) to discern the anchor point placement during my point-by-point build process. I also leverage the shape-building method to create the character's other arm, teeth, wing, tongue, corners of his mouth, and one of the horns. Everything else was created using the point-by-point method.

FIGURE 6.24 This final character design was part of an ad agency pitch for a Fanta Phantom character.

Using both vector build methods will help you master the creation of any shape. Don't let a complex shape intimidate you. Instead, approach it with creative confidence, knowing you can tag-team any vector challenge.

Throw-away Shapes

When you use the shape-building method, you'll create certain shapes for no other reason than to move another shape further along in the build process. These sacrificial shapes are important, but they will never appear in the final art (FIGURES 6.25–6.26).

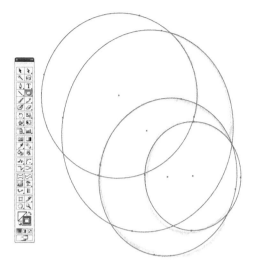

FIGURE 6.25 To create this simple design, start by drawing four circle shapes with the Ellipse tool (L) (shown on the left). Select two shapes at a time and click the Minus Front button within the Pathfinder panel (Shift+Command-F9 or Shift-Control-F9), to form two new shapes (shown on the right). Then create another circular shape, which is our throw-away shape (in blue).

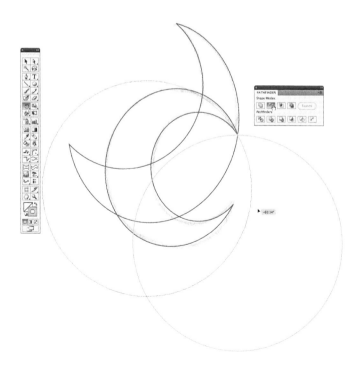

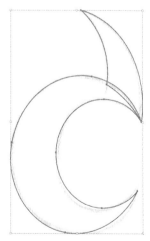

FIGURE 6.26 Using the Rotate tool (R), I position the throw-away shape where I need it (on the left). Next, I select my throw-away shape and my other shape and click the Minus Front button within the Pathfinder panel (Shift-Command-F9 or Shift-Control-F9) to form the final vector shapes needed (shown on the right).

BetterHandles Plug-in

When you create your art using the shape-building method, your final shape might need some additional refining. The BetterHandles plug-in by Nineblock Software can help get that job done.

Remove Redundant Points

As I griped in chapter 2, Adobe Illustrator contains a bug within the Pathfinder panel that creates redundant points in your artwork. This means that one point literally sits on top of another. When you select a shape, it might look normal, but these redundancies can cause problems later.

The BetterHandles plug-in contains a function called Remove Redundant Points that can remove all such duplicate anchor points with a path. Let's take a closer look at how this plug-in works (FIGURE 6.27).

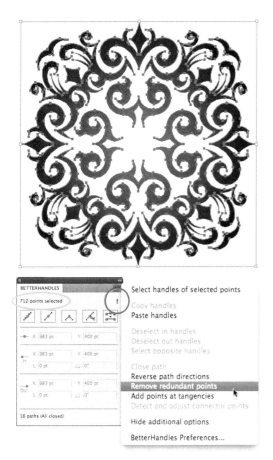

FIGURE 6.27 Select your vector shape. On the BetterHandles panel, you'll see the number of points in your shape on the left (circled in green). If an exclamation mark appears on the right (circled in red here), your art contains redundant points. With your shape still selected, click on the BetterHandles panel and select Remove redundant points. You'll immediately see a new total point count appear on the panel, revealing how many redundant points were removed from your artwork. In this specific case, we removed 14 redundant points.

Smart Remove

Sometimes when you build vector art, whether by the point-by-point or shape-building method, you inevitably add extra points to your vector paths. Or maybe you decide later that you simply don't need one or more of the anchor points you initially placed.

You can use BetterHandles' Smart Remove tool to remove extra anchor points from a path and still retain your art's shape. Let me show you what I mean (FIGURE 6.28).

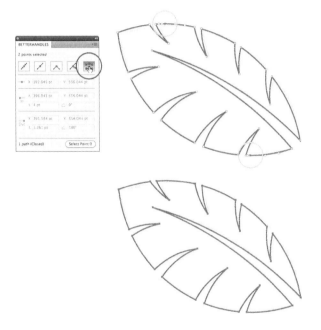

FIGURE 6.28 The final vector shape of the palm leaf motif contains a couple of extra anchor points (circled in green) that we want to remove without jeopardizing the overall shape (see the top palm image). To do this, simply select the problematic anchor points, go to the BetterHandles panel, and click the Smart Remove button (circled in red). Unnecessary anchor points are removed, and your vector shape is retained (bottom image).

E Pluribus Buildum

The phrase "E Pluribus Unum" can be found on United States coinage. It's Latin for "Out of many, one."

This saying can also apply to our creative process as it relates to building vector designs. As you create your vector shapes using either the point-by-point or the shape-building method, you can also benefit by dissecting your design into more manageable individual shapes and then combining them later into the final shape you need.

We touched on this vector building method in chapter 3, and you'll notice it within many of the other images throughout the book as well.

Dissecting Your Design

A variety of complex shapes can make up any design. When it's a custom logotype, for example, the shapes also have to be consistent and precise in order to keep the letterforms readable.

A project like this is made far easier by dissecting your design into smaller individual shapes. This allows you to focus on each part and render it accurately.

By dissecting the shapes shown in FIGURE 6.29 into smaller parts, it helped me maintain the continuity of my content. For example, if you look at the letter H in the word Church in Figure 6.29, I used the horizontal width of its shapes to guide my building on other letterform widths such as the B, U, and R. If I would have tried to build each letterform as one single path, it would have taken a lot more time and effort on my part to pull it off with precision (FIGURES 6.29–6.34).

Whether you're building your design using the point-by-point method or the shape-building method, dissecting your design will work well within a systematic creative process.

FIGURE 6.29 A rough thumbnail sketch of a logotype concept.

FIGURE 6.30 My refined drawing. I'll use this as my guide to build my vector shapes inside my drawing program.

FIGURE 6.31 I focus on individual shapes within my design and dissect them into even smaller individual shapes so that I can build the vector art faster and with more precision.

FIGURE 6.32 This image shows all of the individual shapes that make up this logotype design. To form my final shape, I'll combine the individual shapes using the Pathfinder panel (Shift-Command-F9 or Shift-Control-F9).

FIGURE 6.33 As you progress in the creative process, you should always allow room for improvement. No one is perfect. I noticed areas of my design that could be improved upon. This shows the shapes I'll either add to or subtract from the letterforms to refine the design. We'll go over this in more depth in chapter 8 when we cover "The Fresh Eyes Effect."

FIGURE 6.34 This shows the final logotype design. Note that I removed the inner curls on the C letterforms. This improved the readability and is all part of art directing yourself, which I'll also cover in the chapter 8.

Symmetry Is Your Friend

There's one additional build technique that can be used, in combination with point-by-point and shape-building, that can really speed up your work: working symmetrically.

When you create symmetrical artwork, you only have to build half of the art (top left in FIGURE 6.35). From that you'll be able to create the entire finished piece by simply cloning the shapes you need and flipping them using the Reflect tool.

Here's how:

1. Create your vector art based on your refined sketch. Select your vector shapes (V-Shift). (See the top left of Figure 6.35.)

2. With your vector shapes selected, take the Reflect tool (O) and position it on one of the center anchor points (circled in red). With the Shift key held down, drag the cursor to the left to flip the art. (The flipped vector art is colored green in the top right of Figure 6.35.)

3. Now that you have all of your shapes in place, you'll combine them using the tools in the Pathfinder panel to build your final shape. Just select the various shapes and click the Unite button (if you want to merge shapes) or Minus Front button (if you want to eliminate shapes) to create all of the final vector forms needed for your design (bottom left of Figure 6.35).

The symmetrical character art used the point-by-point method, the shape-building method, and symmetry to create the final design shown at the bottom right of Figure 6.35. The more you're able to combine the various build methods covered in this book, the more productive your workflow will become (FIGURES 6.36–6.45).

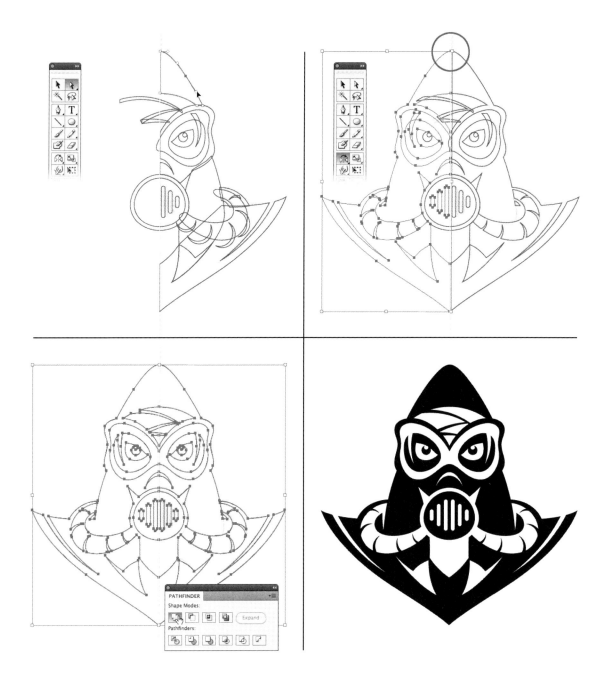

FIGURE 6.35 Profoundly simple symmetrical building can produce simply profound results.

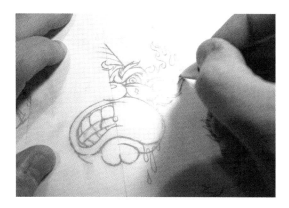

FIGURE 6.36 Drawing the thumbnail sketch for my illustration.

FIGURE 6.37 Refined sketch of illustration. I'll use this as my guide to build my vector shapes inside Illustrator. (Note: The drool at right will not be a symmetrical element.)

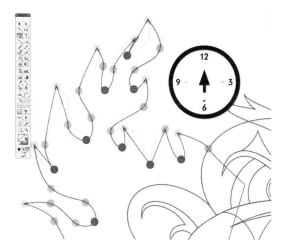

FIGURE 6.38 Using TCM and PPP (covered in chapter 5), I discern my anchor point locations and build my vector art with the point-by-point method to form the flaming hair shape.

FIGURE 6.39 The end result of the four-step point-by-point process renders precise vector art that matches my underlying drawing. I continue to use this methodology as I build the rest of the vector shapes.

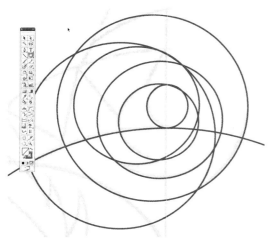

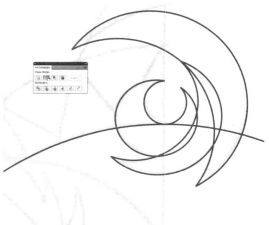

FIGURE 6.40 Using the shape-building method, I create six circular shapes with the Ellipse tool (L) to form part of the hair in my illustration.

FIGURE 6.41 I then select the various shapes and click the Minus Front button within the Pathfinder panel (Shift-Command-F9 or Shift-Control-F9) to knock out the sections of the curve that I don't want to show up in my final graphic. The result is a curved shape that looks more like hair than a circle.

FIGURE 6.42 As I continue to build, I select the shapes and click the Unite function within the Pathfinder panel (Shift-Command-F9 or Shift-Control-F9) along with another throw-away shape to form what makes up the tuft of hair.

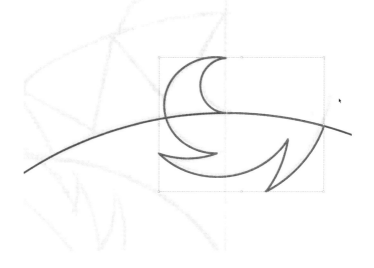

FIGURE 6.43 This image shows all of the final, symmetrically planned shapes that I will clone to complete the final image.

FIGURE 6.44 I clone (Command-C or Control-C, Command-F or Control-F) the vector shapes and flip them using the Reflect tool (O). Once the shapes are reflected, I select various shapes and click the Unite button in the Pathfinder panel (Shift-Command-F9 or Shift-Control-F9) to form all of the vector shapes needed for my final artwork. I remove any redundant or extra anchor points using the BetterHandles plug-in. (Review BetterHandles plug-in instructions covered earlier in this chapter.)

 FIGURE 6.45 I titled the final artwork "Tickles, the Evil Clown." Tickles won several illustration awards, and a large format print was part of a gallery show at the New York Society of Illustrators.

A Healthy Creative Process

I've isolated my various build methods in this chapter so that I could walk you through each one individually. I then explained how to use the methods together in the greater context of a systematic creative process.

But the creative process isn't always as orderly. Many times a project will require you to go back and forth, utilizing earlier methods and applying them later in the creative process in order to arrive at the final vector art needed.

A good example of this back and forth was documented in Figures 3.34–3.36. The same will be true in your own projects as you begin to use the point-by-point method and the shape-building method we covered in this chapter.

A healthy creative process should be flexible, adaptable, and open to the use of any method needed at any given time in order to improve the final result.

FIELD NOTES

Skullduggery

On the DVD, you'll find a file named "Skullduggery.ai" and within this file you'll find eight basic vector shapes:

- 3 Circles

- 3 Rectangles

- 1 Square

- 1 Triangle

Your creative challenge is to take the eight shapes included in the file (you can resize them, but don't distort them) and create a skull graphic using the shape-building method we covered in this chapter.

How did you do? Compare your vector building with this image: http://goo.gl/XVJnh.

DESIGN DRILLS:
Fast and Easy

As we covered earlier in this chapter, dissecting your vector building into smaller, more manageable shapes makes the whole process of forming your art easier and leads to faster build times, especially when you're creating complex designs.

In this section, I've gathered together a few of my more complex designs so you can see how I diced each one up. In each design, I dissected the whole into smaller pieces that were much easier to handle.

FIGURE 6.46 I created this ornament design by dissecting the overall form into multiple shapes. When the various parts are united using the Pathfinder panel, it becomes one big compound path.

FIGURE 6.47 The final ornament shape is duplicated, reflected horizontally using the Reflect tool (O), and then reflected again vertically to form a complete frame motif for a publishing project.

FIGURE 6.48 Whenever you can dissect your work and take advantage of symmetry, you'll slash your build times since you're essentially cutting your workload in half. For example, I only had to create half of the design here. (For more about dissecting, review chapter 6.)

FIGURE 6.49 Tribal bear illustration for St. Martin's Press.

FIGURE 6.50 A complex illustration like this tiger is far easier to flesh out if you dissect the design into smaller, independent shapes. This allows you to work faster while staying focused on the smaller details.

FIGURE 6.51 This tiger illustration was commissioned by a local non-profit for use on an event poster for a diabetes research fundraiser.

CHAPTER 7

Style Appropriate

It's a common misconception in the creative community that you need a signature visual style to gain fame, fortune, and future work. There's no such thing as one-style-fits-all design, and it's unrealistic and inappropriate for you to strangle your creativity with a signature look. Forcing yourself to approach every design project from the same style vantage will actually limit your opportunities and prevent you from growing as a creative person.

As designers, we must study the audience for any project we take on and choose a style for our work that speaks authentically to its members (**FIGURE 7.1**). Your design might be aesthetically pleasing, win numerous awards, and even contain a clever concept, but if it doesn't resonate with its intended audience, it's mere eye candy—delicious, but not very good for you, or your business.

Be creatively proactive and leverage diverse styles in order to produce work that not only meets your clients' needs, but exceeds them. It's an effective way to stay creatively relevant in an ever-changing industry.

> "Failure is not fatal, but failure to change might be."
> — JOHN WOODEN

Design Chameleons

I love expanding my creative horizons by exploring new styles. Being able to work in a variety of styles has resulted in a broader range of projects and clientele. Over the years, I've become a design chameleon of sorts. Many art directors have hired me because I'm able to offer several directions, each in a varying style, in order to help them explore potential solutions.

FIGURE 7.1 (Opposite page, left to right, from top to bottom) Licensing image for Wayne Enterprises, linear line icon for a marketing book, custom logotype for a fencing team, a unique novelty collectible, book cover graphic for St. Martin's Press, and a character design and lettering for a line of beer. Each of the six stylistic choices I used is appropriate for its intended audience.

With each new project, I determine early on what specific style I'll use so I can adequately prepare any reference material I might need. If the style is a more complex one, I determine how long it will take to create and what vector build methods will work best to produce the final art precisely. Having this information gathered before pencil or pen hit the paper is invaluable.

Let's walk through four real-world projects, each of which required me to leverage a very different but appropriate style in order to produce the successful vector artwork my clients needed.

I'm only sharing four specific styles here. Over the years, I've built my creative repertoire to include an ever-growing range of styles, many more than I can share here. Discovering and developing new styles as you progress through your career should be your goal, too.

FIGURE 7.2 Referencing a rough thumbnail, I draw out a refined sketch of the linear line icon.

Linear Line Style

This continuous-line style was initially made popular by Picasso in his sketches and more recently has become a favorite concept within our industry to market everything from insurance, coffee, medical services, real estate, cars and, as demonstrated in this project, banking (FIGURES 7.2–7.14). The linear style is appropriate for this client because it will work for both print collateral and can be easily animated for TV spots.

FIGURE 7.3 Refined sketches of all the linear line icons I'll be creating for an ad agency's banking client. Now that I've drawn out my designs, I know exactly what I need to build in vector form—no guesswork involved. The heavy lifting for this style is done in the drawing stage.

FIGURE 7.4 Most of the linear icons will be created using the point-by-point method, but on this light bulb, I was able to use the shape-building method as well.

FIGURE 7.5 Finessing my Bézier curve to polish off my vector path.

FIGURE 7.6 I determine a nice weight for my final stroke size that will look good when used big or small.

FIGURE 7.7 I had to re-create the bank's logo in the same style of the icons since it would appear in the same context as the icons and type.

FIGURE 7.8 This shows an example of one of the icons, which was created entirely using the point-by-point method.

FIGURE 7.9 The next few images reflect the art direction that is often required by clients. In this case, they wanted the nose rounded off.

FIGURE 7.10 The client also requested that the mouth span the whole face, so I edited my vector art to make this change.

FIGURE 7.11 At this point, the client didn't like one of the eyes and also asked that the loop in the nose be removed. Overall, the changes were reasonable and I think they improved the final icon, which is the whole point of art direction.

FIGURE 7.12 The client decided another icon of a hand was needed, so I quickly sketched out this concept.

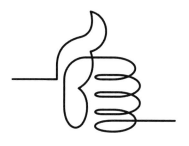

FIGURE 7.13 The final linear line hand, giving a thumbs-up.

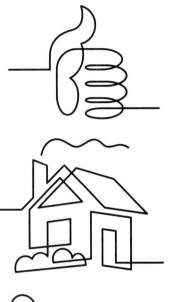

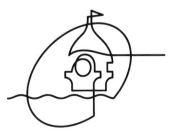

FIGURE 7.14 This linear line style lends itself to animation in which the line draws itself. That's exactly how the agency used it with TV spot advertisements for the banks. It was also utilized in print collateral pieces and signage within the banks, too.

Segmented Style

If I have a signature style that is more readily recognized as "Von," it would be this one. Like many illustrators, I was heavily influenced by the work of Jim Flora, a 1950s art director at RCA Records, to whose work my segmented style gives his work a subtle nod. I've worked in this style on projects for Adobe, a national restaurant chain, a book publisher, magazines, and, in this example, a self-promotional product I created called Keyboard Characters. I used the segmented style on this self-promotional item because I wanted to secure more assignments that would require the style (FIGURES 7.15–7.26).

FIGURE 7.15 My thumbnail sketches for a keyboard character called "Riled Rover," from a larger set of self-promotional items.

FIGURE 7.16 My refined sketch for Riled Rover. Sometimes I re-draw something and tape it on top of a previous iteration, as I've done here.

FIGURE 7.17 My frankensteined but refined sketch is ready to be scanned in and used.

FIGURE 7.18 Most of my vector paths are built using the point-by-point method; I keep The Clockwork Method (TCM) in mind as I place my anchor points. But on the teeth, I used the shape-building method via the Ellipse tool (L) and the Pathfinder panel (Command-Shift-F9 or Control-Shift-F9).

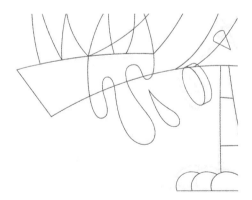

FIGURE 7.19 Notice how I build my vector art to match my drawing. The only areas where I deviate from my drawing are the pieces that are easier build in digital, such as the spikes, dog tag, and the toes, all of which I created using the shape-building tools in Illustrator.

FIGURE 7.20 All of my base vector shapes are now complete.

FIGURE 7.21 I begin to work out all of my flat fill colors.

FIGURE 7.22 My final art for the Riled Rover keyboard character.

FIGURE 7.23 These are three more keyboard characters in the set: Pet Monster, DZGN-BOT, and Feed Your Imagination.

FIGURE 7.24 Press proof for the keyboard character set.

FIGURE 7.25 Color proof for the Riled Rover keyboard character.

FIGURE 7.26 The finished keyboard characters self-promotional product.

Tribal Tattoo Style

A few years back, a group of illustrators, including me, would meet once a month, and each of us would illustrate our own take on an agreed-upon topic. One month it was tattoos. I've always liked the graphic nature of tribal tattoos so I decided to draw a face.

Because of that simple creative exploration, I can now utilize this style for such client projects as book covers, custom tattoo designs, energy drinks, stickers, and, as you'll see in **FIGURES 7.27–7.47**, a poster design for the Rock and Roll Hall of Fame. The tribal tattoo style is appropriate for this product because the nature of the client and its story are more extreme. This style was able to communicate that well.

FIGURE 7.27 My thumbnail sketch for the poster design.

FIGURE 7.28 Whenever I'm unfamiliar with a topic, I'll research it and pull reference images together so that what I'm creating is accurate for the intended audience (who's likely much more expert than me on the topic). I'm pretty clueless when it comes to music, so I studied the shape of guitars before I began drawing my design.

FIGURES 7.29 and **7.30** Using a previous tribal illustration I had created as inspiration, I start drawing out my tribal art in the shape of a guitar. I draw my art out on vellum and make changes as I go until I have the precise drawn form I need.

FIGURE 7.31 This shows my refined sketch for the guitar portion of my design. At this point, I draw out the neck of the guitar two different ways, not sure of which way I'll end up going.

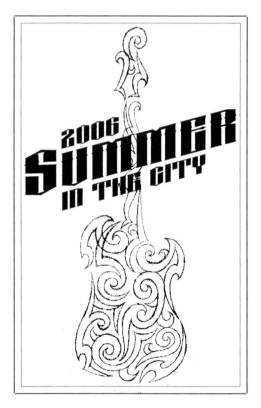

FIGURE 7.32 I scan in my drawing and do a rough layout composite to get the overall spacing and proportions nailed down.

FIGURE 7.33 I print out my rough composite and then refine my art, drawing out the remaining design content such as the flames.

FIGURE 7.34 I begin to build my vector artwork using the point-by-point method. The tribal style is easier than most to build. Since the art has a lot of areas that come to a point, it's easy to discern the anchor point placement.

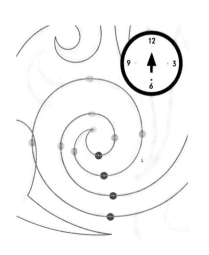

FIGURE 7.36 I keep TCM in mind as I create all of the curved shapes in my tribal design.

FIGURE 7.35 As you can see, I follow my refined sketch closely. There's not a lot of guesswork at this stage, just following what I've already determined via my scanned refined sketch.

FIGURES 7.37 and 7.38 As I progress digitally with my design (at left), I like to print it out and scrutinize the art, looking for any areas that may contain visual tension or just might look better if revised (above). This type of self art direction is a vital part of a systematic creative process.

FIGURE 7.39 I build out all of my base vector shapes for the poster design and double-check for any areas of visual tension that need to be addressed. I make several tweaks to the flame vectors around the type and base of the guitar. You can see these improvements wherever the vector art doesn't align with my original drawing.

FIGURE 7.40 I begin to explore color themes. Note how I made the call to lose the detailing inside the letterforms. It was just drawing too much attention, so I simplified the letters, which helped the overall readability.

FIGURE 7.41 Many times vector art looks too perfect, too clean, and, in this case, I thought the design warranted a distressed look and feel. To accomplish this, I simply used a roll of duct tape, a hard-edged ruler, and a printout (either inkjet or laser will work) that contained a solid, large area of black toner.

FIGURE 7.42 I crumpled the printout so it started to flake off toner, leaving specks and streaks. Then I balled up some duct tape and started tapping the surface, randomly removing toner to form an authentic distressed look.

FIGURE 7.43 I folded the printout and scraped the edge of the fold with my straight-edged ruler. This removed more toner and created nice crease marks that spanned the surface. I rotated the page and varied the angles to add interest and authenticity to the texturing.

FIGURE 7.44 The finished distressed printout, ready to scan in.

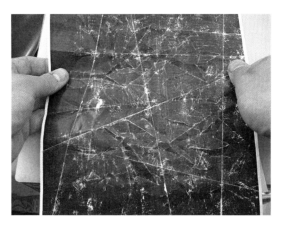

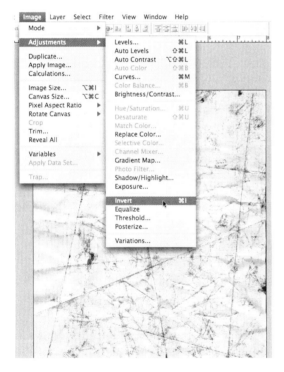

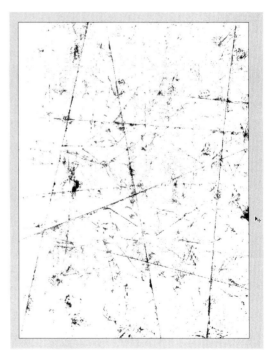

FIGURES 7.45 and 7.46 I scanned in the image as a grayscale TIFF and, within Photoshop, inverted the scan (Image > Adjustments > Invert) to create a positive TIFF image. I then placed the image into my vector file and positioned it on the topmost layer. This gives my final design an authentic distressed look.

LIVE AT THE ROCK AND ROLL HALL OF FAME AND MUSEUM

FREE concerts
on Key Plaza.

Wednesday's
from 6pm — 9pm
outside stage
If weather does not permit -
we will move inside.

July 12 The Giraffes
The Vacation

July 26
Electric Six
Dirty Americans
Amps II Eleven
With special appearance from
the Burning River Roller Girls.

August 9
The Whigs
Dreadful Reeds
A combination of the Dreadful
Yawns and the New Lou Reeds.
Blake Miller

August 23
The Sun
Tim Easton
Chris Allen

www.rockhall.com

2006 SUMMER IN THE CITY

FIGURE 7.47 The final Rock and Roll Hall of Fame poster design utilizing the tribal tattoo style.

Graphic Style

Not all projects require an extensive illustrative approach. A simple and iconic style can be more appropriate for such projects as custom lettering, icons, ornaments, or a logo design for an Italian animation company (**FIGURES 7.48–7.58**). Keeping the style simple means that this logo can be more easily adapted to a broad range of applications without running into readability problems.

But the main reason I picked this stylistic direction is because it adheres to my design philosophy regarding logo identity: Simple is better.

FIGURE 7.48 I rough out my symmetrical thumbnail for the logo design, scan it in, and mock up the whole face so I can sketch out my type. ("Bocca" means "mouth" in Italian.) I'll use this rough version to draw my refined sketch from.

FIGURE 7.49 Guided by my rough composite (shown in Figure 7.48), I draw out my refined sketch. Since the design is symmetrical, I'll only have to build half of the character's face.

FIGURE 7.50 I find three areas where the spacing between the elements is too tight, which creates visual tension. So I'll be sure to balance out those areas as I move forward. (See chapter 8 for more about visual tension.)

FIGURE 7.51 The majority of this design is created using the point-by-point method. A few spots, like the nostril and pupil of the eye, were created using the shape-building method.

FIGURES 7.52–7.54 Now that I have all of my symmetrical vectors created, I select all of the shapes and flip them using the Reflect tool (O) to form my final base vector artwork.

FIGURE 7.55 I now work out my color scheme for the logo.

FIGURES 7.56 and 7.57 Small, seemingly insignificant details can add a lot to a design. On this logo design, just adding the small hot spots (white circles) to the eyes breathes life into this logo. These are the small improvements you should look for as you art direct yourself while creating your work.

FIGURE 7.58 Final Big Bocca logo design using a simple iconic style.

FIELD NOTES

Create a Style Board

A simple creative habit that will help you recognize appropriate styles for various genres is to take notice of them in other contexts. I encourage you to start collecting samples of various styles you come across and build a style board with them.

A bulletin board in your work area or office is a convenient place to hang up different styles you like and might want to try in your own work. With an established collection, you won't forget about particular styles, and the board will build your creative confidence as you move forward.

A smart designer will leverage various styles in order to be a more effective visual communicator. If you find yourself stuck in the same old visual rut, then move in a new direction. Try a completely different style on your next project instead of creatively capitulating to the same tired routine.

DESIGN DRILLS:
Use It or Lose It

A systematic creative process in which you draw out an idea, refine it, and then build it in vector form—making continual improvements and needed adjustments along the way—is only successful if it's a process that you apply consistently on every project.

In other words, if you don't use the methods covered in this book routinely, as in *every day*, then you won't see the ultimate benefits over time. Use it or lose it; it's up to you.

The character design project that I'm about to show you here uses the methods I've outlined in this book, all of which are essential to establishing a useful and repeatable creative process.

FIGURE 7.59 Thumbnail sketches of Mickey the Rat character design.

FIGURE 7.60 Dialing in the character more through a tighter rough sketch.

FIGURE 7.61 Further refinement of my character design. I drew the body and head separately so I could play around with the positioning.

FIGURE 7.62 The finalized refined sketch that I'll scan in and use to build my vector shapes.

FIGURE 7.63 For most of this design, I'll utilize the point-by-point method, which is described in chapter 6, but I decided to use the shape-building method (also in chapter 6) to create the tongue. It will take four ellipse shapes to create it.

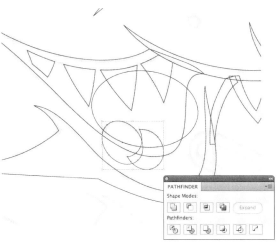

FIGURE 7.64 From the Pathfinder panel, I select the ellipse shapes and begin to build out the tongue.

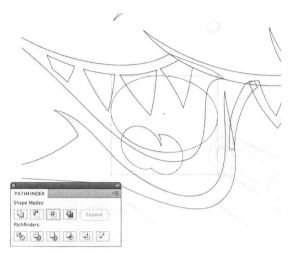

FIGURE 7.65 I now have only two shapes remaining, so I'll select both and click Intersect in the Pathfinder panel (highlighted in green)

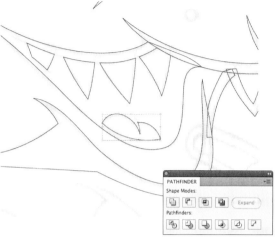

FIGURE 7.66 The final tongue shape, formed entirely with the shape-building method.

FIGURE 7.67 At this point, I have all of the base vector shapes for the head completed.

FIGURE 7.68 I do a rough build of the cigarette smoke. I don't worry about fine-tuning the Bézier curves at this point. I'm more concerned about the proper point placements.

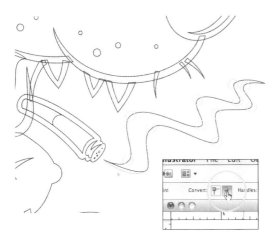

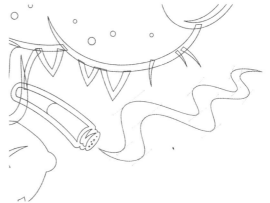

FIGURE 7.69 I use the Xtream Path plug-in to tweak my vector path so that it's closer to the final shape I'll need. Then, I select all of the anchor points that need to be smooth anchor points (circled in green) and click the "Convert selected anchor points to smooth" button in the Control panel at the top-left side of the screen.

FIGURE 7.70 With the anchor points now smooth, I extend the Bézier handles to form the elegant curves that will make up the smoke shape.

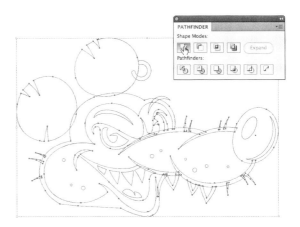

FIGURE 7.71 All of my base vector shapes for this character design are now complete. At this stage, I like to save a copy of all of the vector paths on a new layer, just to be safe. Only then do I continue.

FIGURE 7.72 I select all of the vector shapes that make up the head and, in the Pathfinder panel, click Unite to fuse them together to form the final head.

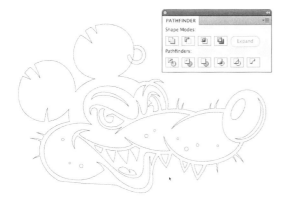

FIGURE 7.73 I now have the basis of the final artwork for the character's head.

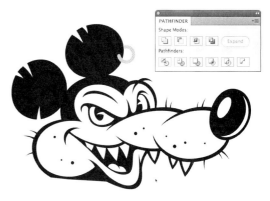

FIGURE 7.74 I flesh out the black and white so I can study the form of my art's shape easier when I print it out.

FIGURE 7.75 I follow the same procedures described earlier to create the character's body and then print it. Now is the time to art direct myself. On the print-outs, I note areas where I need to improve details and refine my vector artwork even more.

FIGURE 7.76 After vector art refinements are made, I can begin to play with color. I never touch color until all of my base shapes and form are completely dialed in.

FIGURE 7.77 It's time to leverage drawing once again. I print out my colored art and begin to draw in the shading for the character using a simple 2B pencil. Remember: The process is both analog and digital throughout the creative process.

FIGURE 7.78 I like to use a red felt-tip pen to draw out where the highlighting should be.

FIGURE 7.79 Final Mickey Rat character illustration.

CHAPTER 8

Art Directing Yourself

There's a plethora of creative people in the communication arts industry. And we all compete with each other in a global marketplace, with the Internet serving as an ever-present facilitator. Design opinions shift quickly, trends take flight, and we can showcase our work to more people worldwide than ever before.

The quality of work produced by this legion of designers covers the gamut from horrible to heavenly. What separates the best from the rest in this graphic cacophony is often the individual's ability to scrutinize his or her own work earnestly, admit its shortcomings, revise the creative process, and improve his or her capabilities with each new project. In other words, the artist must know how to self-art direct.

Art direction isn't so much about correcting mistakes as it is about shaping perceptions. When you art direct yourself, your goal is to craft an aesthetic that achieves a desired response from a given audience.

Think of it this way: Design tends to be a wonderful paradox where objective methods produce creative work that is viewed subjectively.

Fresh Eyes Effect

Creative people spend so much time looking at their work that it can be very difficult to notice potential problems. Everything begins to blend together. When this happens, honest critique is missed, and with it, needed improvements.

This is a dangerous situation because it can result in subpar work. It also opens the door for your client to notice problems and directly associate that lack of attention to detail with you as a creative person.

A simple method to help you avoid this situation is to use what I call the "fresh eyes effect." As you reach various stages in your work, set it aside and work on something completely different for a while. An hour is ideal, but even 15 minutes can be enough to purge your mind's cache and refresh your eyes. When you reapproach your work later, you can scrutinize it with *fresh eyes*, allowing you to see areas you can improve upon. What you'll need to improve and the degree of improvements or tweaks you'll need to make will be different for each person depending on your ability and what stage of the creative process the work is in.

When I was hired by a beverage company to illustrate a tribal tattoo-styled Aztec warrior, I first drew out my refined sketch as shown in

FIGURE 8.1 My initial refined sketch for the tribal tattoo-styled Aztec warrior.

FIGURE 8.2 A new refined sketch derived from the fresh eyes effect.

FIGURE 8.1. I spent a lot of time working on this, but something just didn't feel right. Whenever that happens, it's a sign for me to set the project down, walk away, and reapproach it with fresh eyes later. So I shelved the job and decided to pick it up again the next day.

The next morning, I looked at my initial refined sketch with fresh eyes and was able to pinpoint the problematic attributes within my art. After reviewing my drawing, the proportion of the overall head seemed too thin, the ethnicity didn't look correct either, and the eyes were getting lost in the detail, so they weren't as captivating as they could be. I made the needed corrections to my refined sketch and the overall result was an authentic vibe the previous sketch was missing (FIGURE 8.2).

With my refined sketch dialed in, I was able to get it approved by my client and move forward with building the design in vector form (FIGURE 8.3).

FIGURE 8.3 Building the vector shapes, using TCM, PPP, and other techniques outlined in chapters 5 and 6.

FIGURE 8.4 Final vector artwork used on the packaging of an energy drink. Fresh eyes helped me create work that served my client better.

In a creative environment that demands an accelerated timeline, perhaps using fresh eyes can seem unrealistic. But I'd argue it's not impossible. Even allowing yourself a small amount of time to reset your creative perspective is better than none at all (**FIGURE 8.4**).

Your Inner Art Director

Self-art direction isn't limited to the drawing stage of a systematic creative process. It can also take place during the building stage of your vector creation.

A responsible designer should always be looking for the opportunity to improve and grow creatively. Part of this growth comes from paying proper attention to detail as you progress through the creative process on any given project.

Listen to your inner art director and be sensitive to those sometimes-fleeting feelings that subtly reveal themselves to you as you work. Don't ignore them—correct the problems that they uncover. The project shown in FIGURES 8.5–8.13 utilizes many of the methods we've covered in this book so far. Along the way, however, my inner art director took notice of areas in my art I could improve upon (FIGURE 8.8).

In chapter 3, I made the case for why you must depend on both analog and digital methods to create your vector art (Figures 3.34–3.36). In this project, the same balance of analog and digital apply. Once I have my base vector art in place, as shown in FIGURE 8.7, I will print out a black-and-white version and begin to draw out my shading detail (Figure 8.8). I'll eventually scan this back in and use it as my road map to build the vector shapes that form the shading in my final design (Figures 8.12–8.13).

As I was drawing out the shading detail, something about the form of the bottom half of the alien skull was bugging me. My inner art director pinpointed the problem areas at the base of the skull, which was too narrow and which made the shape of my design somewhat awkward. (Figure 8.8). It's important to remember that art direction like this is subjective, for the most part. This area of my art isn't necessarily wrong; it's just not as aesthetically effective or pleasing as it could be. In other words, there was room for improvement, so I made revisions (Figures 8.9–8.11).

FIGURE 8.5 Thumbnail sketches for an alien skull design commissioned by a UK publisher.

FIGURE 8.6 My refined alien skull sketch on left (note that I'm working symmetrically) and my vector build shown on right.

FIGURE 8.7 This shows the entire base vector art built. I'll now print it out in black and white so I can draw out my shading.

FIGURE 8.8 I revert to analog mode and draw out my shading detail. I'll eventually scan this back in and build my vector shapes from it for shading. As I was shading, my inner art director noticed the areas that could use improvement (circled here in red).

FIGURE 8.9 This is the area that I felt could be improved. It looked too thin and the shading here contradicted my approach elsewhere in the design.

FIGURE 8.10 I reshaped the vectors on the bottom half of the alien skull to improve its overall appearance.

FIGURE 8.11 I continued to create the new vector shapes needed to match the shading style of my design.

FIGURE 8.12 I built all of the shading shapes based on the drawing that I scanned back in. All that is left now is to finalize my color.

FIGURE 8.13 The final alien skull design that benefited directly from self-art direction.

I could have just let the art stand and not made any of these changes, but I think revising the shape of the skull as well as the added shading helped to make the end product a stronger piece of artwork. This, of course, is my opinion. Art direction tends to be subjective, but it's these types of small refinements that you want to make throughout the creative process to ensure your designs are consistently produced at the highest level possible. In other words, don't settle for good enough: If you think you can improve something, that's a good enough excuse to do it (FIGURE 8.13).

Making small, continual improvements to your work over the entire span of a given project is a sure sign of a healthy creative process.

No one's work is perfect when it hits the page. As you work with others during your career, they'll no doubt point out problems in your work that you're blind to. Don't take offense; it's important to absorb all forms of art direction so you can learn, grow, and become the best you can possibly be.

The fact that you're reading this book reveals that you are well-equipped to accept this sort of input, and that's a good sign.

Avoid Visual Tension

Shape is important when creating vector artwork. But how a shape relates to another shape within any given design context is of equal or even greater importance. You might produce a well-crafted and precise shape, but if it's not balanced well with other shapes, it will suffer aesthetically. I define this type of problematic shape relationship as visual tension.

Look at FIGURE 8.14. Where does your eye automatically go when you look at these shapes? Likely, your eye will naturally return to the area circled in red in FIGURE 8.15 because that is where visual tension exists.

FIGURE 8.14 Look at this graphic and let your eye naturally go where it wants to go.

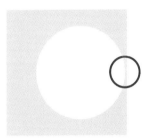

FIGURE 8.15 If you're like most people, your eye zeroed in on the location circled in red. The circle is too close to the edge of the square. Visual tension exists because the shape relationship between the square and circle isn't a balanced one.

FIGURE 8.16 You can remove the visual tension by moving the circle further away from the square's edge, adding balance to the relationship.

FIGURE 8.17 You can also remove the visual tension by moving the circle further past the square's edge so it clearly overlaps it and improves the shape relationship.

The tension is caused because the circle is too close to the edge of the green square. It unintentionally draws the eye to that area. To remedy this, you have to either move the circle further away from the edge as shown in FIGURE 8.16, or move the circle past the edge as shown in FIGURE 8.17.

Most successful designers are expert manipulators, practiced in the art of using composition to visually guide a viewer's eye through a design or to focus attention on a specific location within a given context. This type of viewer response is what you want, a purposeful attention to important content that is not distracted by unnecessary or poor design.

Bad design, in general, is riddled with visual tension. The more areas of visual tension within a graphic, the more it runs the risk of compromising the intended visual communication. It's crucial, as a self-art director, to recognize and remove visual tension from your artwork. And, as with anything, the first step in solving a problem is recognizing that you have one.

Recognize Visual Tension

Before we jump into a real-world project that contains visual tension, let's take a look at a common graphic that everyone is familiar with, the American flag. I think it's safe to say we've all seen this image enough that we could spot anything in it that is not quite right.

If you look at FIGURE 8.18, you'll see a normal flag and one with a lot of visual tension. Can you pinpoint all 22 areas of visual tension in this graphic? Some problems are obvious, whereas some are much more subtle.

I should point out that sometimes a designer wants to purposely mess up a graphic in order to achieve a certain look and feel. In that context, visual tension is thrown out the window and really doesn't apply at all. But that's the exception, not the rule. So unless the genre specifically calls for a style that is loose, random, or chaotic in its composition, visual tension should be viewed as a negative attribute within a design.

The flag samples demonstrate that visual tension can be both overt and subtle. The latter is the harder to spot, so you'll really need to train your eye so you can detect visual tension in any piece of artwork.

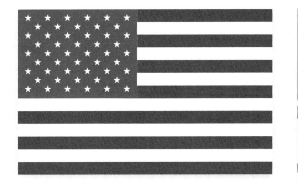 

FIGURE 8.18   There is a total of 22 areas of visual tension in the right flag graphic. Eight stars are either positioned or scaled wrong; the blue background is shifted and distorted; six of the seven red stripes are either positioned, distorted, or scaled wrong; and there are seven white stripes that are either positioned, distorted, or scaled wrong.

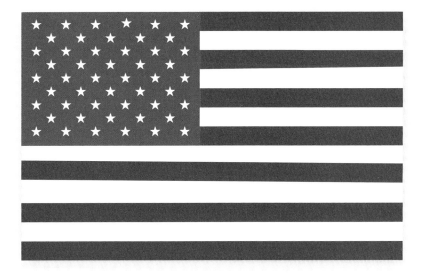

FIGURE 8.19   We've corrected 19 of the 22 areas of visual tension in the flag graphic. But three subtle areas of visual tension remain. Can you pinpoint them? (One star is positioned wrong, and two of the red stripes are distorted or positioned wrong.)

FIGURE 8.20 The logotype contains numerous areas of visual tension.

Let me walk you through one of my projects in which I isolated several instances of visual tension so you can see how I resolved them.

When I added the various outlines to this hand-lettered logotype, it caused a lot of visual tension (FIGURE 8.20). Look closely and you'll see:

A. The descender of the letter K is too thin.

B. The letter U is sitting on the edge of the letter K.

C. The letter S is touching the edge of the letter U.

D. The letter S was obstructing too much of the letter U.

E. There is too much space between the letter S and the letter K.

F. Both arms of the letter K are too thin.

G. The letter K should overlap the letter O.

H. The exclamation mark is too thin and short.

Visual tension can be caused by any sort of poorly handled shape relationship. Any time your eye is pulled toward an unintended area, it's a safe bet that there is some form of visual tension within the design.

With the visual tension areas identified, we can fix them (FIGURE 8.21). Notice how I also fixed the awkward slivers of negative space created by the outlines around the letters "U" and "S."

FIGURE 8.21 Compare the before and after of this logotype. We've removed all areas of visual tension from the bottom sample to bring a nice balance to our design. Spotting visual tension may at first seem a bit foreign to you, but over time you'll develop the eye to spot these problems so you can correct them.

FIGURE 8.22 Final vector artwork used on packaging for a line of kid's snacks. I paid very close attention when I added in the bear character so as not to create new areas of visual tension within the final design.

Full-Tilt Creative Boogie

If creativity has an antithesis, it has to be complacency.

In order to grow as a creative person, it's essential to leave your comfort zone to try new things, take some design risks, be willing to apply new methods like the fresh eyes effect, and catch and fix visual tension, all while you develop new styles for yourself and your clients.

Realize that when you do these things, you're bound to fail, but that only adds to your growth.

Art directing yourself means you need to be your worst critic. Don't settle for good enough. Keep your creative standard high and relentlessly pursue design excellence as often as possible so it becomes your new creative normal.

Resist taking the easy road toward stagnation. Instead, stir up your creative juices and eventually you'll be doing the full-tilt creative boogie!

DESIGN DRILLS:
Hop to It

Nothing teaches methodology like redundancy and also redundancy. We're going to walk through yet another design project in order to cement the entire vector creative process in your brain.

This time, let's take a gander at another character illustration project called "Thug Bunny" and see what methods are utilized to create the final vector artwork.

FIGURE 8.23 We begin by drawing out thumbnail sketches of our character, Thug Bunny. Step away from your computer, people, and pick up the pencil and paper. Sketching out your ideas before you head into Illustrator is essential to creating precise illustrations.

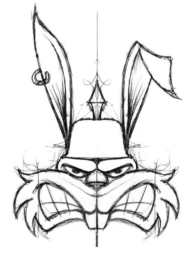

FIGURE 8.24 Dialing the character in more with a tighter rough sketch. I drew only half of the art, scanned it, and then flipped it to gauge if I was moving in the right direction.

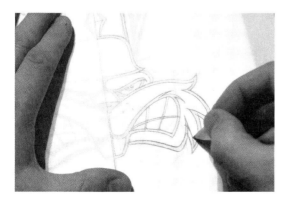

FIGURE 8.25 Using the tighter rough sketch as my guide, I now draw out my refined sketch.

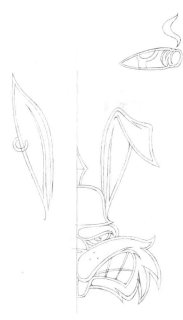

FIGURE 8.27 Rough building on the character's face. The only thing I'm concerned about here is placing the anchor points in their correct positions. I proceed point by point (see chapter 6).

FIGURE 8.26 This is the finalized sketch, which I'll scan in and use to build my vector shapes. Don't forget that we'll rely on our good friend symmetry to complete the picture.

FIGURE 8.28 With my anchor points in their correct PPP, I use the Xtream path plug-in to shape my Bézier curves, adjusting the handles so that the curves match those in my underlying sketch.

FIGURE 8.29 Notice how I dissected my design into smaller, more manageable, shapes. Now I'll use the Pathfinder panel (Shift-Command-F9 or Shift-Control-F9) to Unite (highlighted in green) my vector shapes.

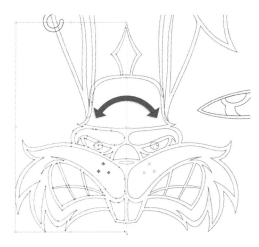

FIGURE 8.30 With all of my base vector shapes completed, I copy them and use the Reflect tool to flip them. (For more information on using symmetry, see chapter 6.)

FIGURE 8.31 Once I've fused all of the elements together, I'm ready to start filling in my design with black and white.

FIGURE 8.32 With my black and white filled in, I scrutinize my design, looking for areas I can improve upon. Sometimes I print out the art and mark it up with a red pen, but on this project, my scrutiny was onscreen only.

FIGURE 8.33 I notice areas of visual tension.

FIGURE 8.34 I remove both areas of visual tension simply by moving the cigar shape down. (For more information on visual tension, review chapter 8.)

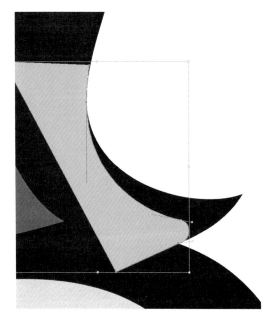

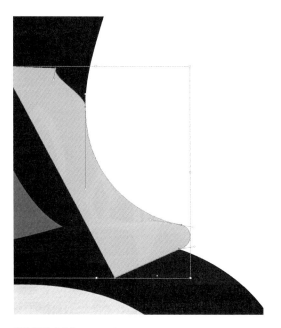

FIGURE 8.35 After walking away from the project for a few hours and returning with fresh eyes, I notice that the brim of the helmet comes to too much of a point, so I rebuild that part (shown in green).

FIGURE 8.36 I modify my black-and-white art and Unite this new piece (colored green) to it via the Pathfinder panel. (For more information about Pathfinder, review chapter 2.)

FIGURE 8.37 This image shows the helmet before the necessary edit.

FIGURE 8.38 This image shows the helmet after.

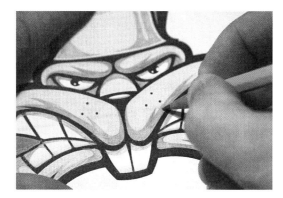

FIGURE 8.39 Time to jump back into analog. At this point, I print out my character design and draw in the shading details.

FIGURE 8.40 I'll scan this drawn shading in and use it as a guide from which to build in Illustrator.

FIGURE 8.41 Like my initial refined sketch, this shading serves as my guide.

FIGURE 8.42 As I was nearing the end of this project, I thought the helmet looked too bare, so I sketched out a logo idea and then built it. After all, Thug Bunny wouldn't be half as cool if he didn't have his own brand logo to emblazon on his helmet.

FIGURE 8.43 Final Thug Bunny character illustration.

CHAPTER 9

Good Creative Habits

Whether you're a designer or an illustrator, you're expected to deliver creativity on a daily basis. It doesn't matter if you're in the mood to create or not. You rarely have the luxury of simply waiting until inspiration strikes to move forward on a design project.

So how do you stay on creative high alert, armed and ready to meet your impending daily design challenges? The answer is simple: establish good creative habits (FIGURE 9.1).

Good creative habits help to increase productivity, improve efficiency, raise quality, fuel creative passion, ignite inspiration, bring about new creative opportunities, cure cancer, solve homelessness, and establish ever-lasting peace on Earth. OK, well, maybe not those last three things.

In this chapter, I will share several creative habits that I use regularly and find effective. I strongly encourage you to try them out. I also want you to remain constantly on the hunt for new creative habits that are specific

FIGURE 9.1 The good creative habit of doodling can be leveraged as final art, as shown in this editorial illustration called "Digital Lifestyle."

to *your* work as you move forward in your career. Strive to continually establish good creative habits and stick with them, and your well of inspiration will never run dry.

"A moment's insight is sometimes worth a life's experience."
— OLIVER WENDELL HOLMES

Doodle Binders

All designers should draw—period.

The systematic creative processes that I've documented throughout this book all illustrate the importance of sound drawing skills in building precise vector graphics. And in chapter 3, I show how drawing can help you better formulate ideas and expand your creative potential. That's not to say that all designers should strive to be illustrators. But doodling on a regular basis is a great way to flex those drawing muscles and develop them into a new and powerful part of your creative approach. Draw, draw, draw—everywhere, anywhere, all the time.

So, the first creative habit that I want you to add to your routine is doodling. Doodling works best when done spontaneously, without any pretext. That said, to sustain and capture this type of random creative energy, you need to plan ahead. Here are some simple things you can do to establish effective doodling skills.

1. **Keep pen and paper handy:** Whether it's a moleskin sketchbook or just a notepad, keep it next to you at work, in your living room, in your car, when you travel, next to the phone, in your purse, and so on. You need to be able to draw at a moment's notice. As long as you have a pen, though, you can draw on anything. I do it all of the time (**FIGURE 9.2**).

FIGURE 9.2 **You can doodle on anything. This styrofoam cup served the purpose well and was created by my daughter Savannah. (Of course, I take full genetic credit for this creativity.)**

2. **Save your doodles:** Whenever you draw a new doodle, make sure you save it. I like to cut mine out of the paper I drew it on (I prefer doodling on notepads), and file it in what I call my doodle folder (**FIGURE 9.3**).

FIGURE 9.3 I save all of my doodles no matter what I draw them on and keep them until needed in a designated doodle folder.

3. **Archive your doodles:** Once your doodle folder nears overflowing, it's time to move your doodles to a more permanent home. I take the ones I've collected, paste them on regular bond paper, slide them into plastic sleeves, and insert these pages into a doodle binder.

Over a period of time, you can create an incredible doodle reference library that documents your own spontaneous and random inspiration. My own doodle binders date back over 20 years now, and when I look through them, I re-live the creative thoughts I had at that time (FIGURE 9.4). I've also used old ideas years later that would otherwise have long been forgotten if not for this single good creative habit.

Besides the practical benefits of doodling and saving your doodles, it's also just a whole lot of fun! That reason alone should support my argument for making it a habitual creative priority.

Layers Are Your Friend

I love teaming up with other designers on creative projects. The brainstorming and conceptual partnership involved in working together toward one common goal makes for a great experience and, more importantly, it results in incredible design solutions.

The proverbial fly in this collaborative ointment for me, however, usually involves the differences in creative habits—specifically how other designers organize their files and manage their graphic content.

By the time the collaborative process is done and a fellow designer sends me his or her final art, I already know what to expect, since I viewed comps of it during the creative process. So all I need at that point is access to the vector art files.

Many times, though, when I open up the vector file, I see vector art that, while it looks good to the naked eye, is so horribly built that using it is not just difficult, but painful.

I admit that I'm a bit anal retentive when it comes to my file management, but there really is no excuse for not using layers and for failing to organize vector content properly. That's just lazy building, which begs trouble down the road.

FIGURE 9.4 I take all of my collected doodles and archive them in doodle binders for easy referencing and for safekeeping. The binders are also a great resource for inspiration.

What type of trouble? Here are a few problematic scenarios that non-layered design files might spawn:

1. **Build Time:** If you layer your design as you progress with each new part of the whole, you'll save yourself a lot of time later hunting and pecking to isolate content within the design. Using layers not only speeds up your build times, but it also makes any later editing far easier. Using layers also gives you better control over vector blend mode hierarchy, so you can get the visual effect you're after. (For more on layering and how it assists in organizing and utilizing blend modes, deconstruct the resource file for chapter 6 on the DVD called "Tickles the Evil Clown.")

2. **Clutter:** Avoiding layers suggests that you're trying to see everything all the time as you create your vector design, which can become a distraction on a complex project. Being able to focus on a specific element within your design, without other content getting in the way, will make for better focus. If you use layers, accessing only the content you need at any given time will be less confusing because you can use layers to simply toggle to make content visible or not visible.

3. **Repurposing:** It's a huge hassle to reuse unlayered vector art in future work. Trying to pinpoint specific vector shapes and select them will be frustrating. The user also runs the risk of missing some of the necessary content when he or she tries to copy vector art to another file because some crucial items might be hiding under an element that isn't needed. Layering content helps you to avoid these types of problems.

4. **Retrieval:** How many pieces of art do you create within a given year? Will you remember exactly how you constructed a complex design when it's been five years since you last opened the file? More than likely, you won't, and you'll waste time trying to deconstruct the art in order to use it. Layering the art properly allows you to see exactly how the work was built.

As you build your design, think of ways to logically organize your vector content. This will help you build files that are easy to navigate so that you can find the vector elements you need quickly.

Let's take a look at a few projects and see how layering plays a vital role in the overall creative process (**FIGURES 9.5–9.17B**).

FIGURE 9.5 Thumbnail sketch for a caricature illustration of President Barack Obama.

FIGURE 9.6 My refined symmetrical caricature sketch is done, and I'll now scan it in and move from analog into digital, building my vector shapes on top of the sketch in my drawing program. (For more information on drawing, review chapter 3. For more information about using symmetry, review chapter 6.)

FIGURE 9.7 I'll use both the point-by-point method (shown at top) and the shape-building method (shown below) to create my vector art.

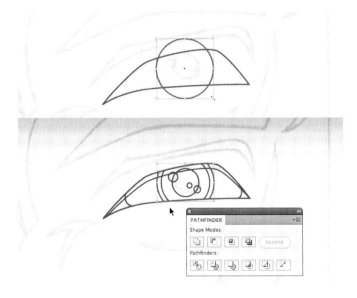

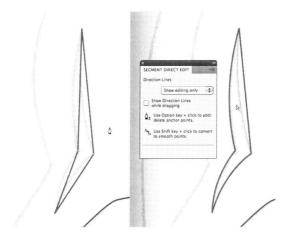

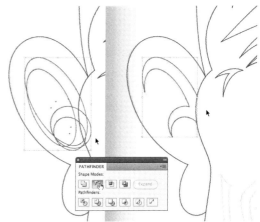

FIGURE 9.8 Using the Xtream Path plug-in (CValley Software), I form my vector shapes to match my underlying refined sketch.

FIGURE 9.9 Any time I can use a shape tool like the Ellipse tool (L) to create my content with precision, I do so because it's faster than the point-by-point method on these types of geometric shapes.

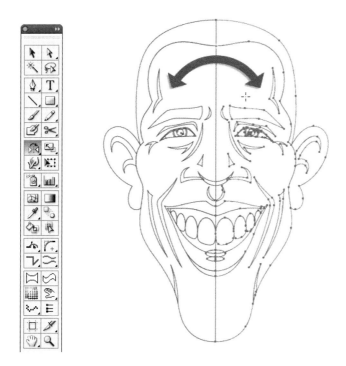

FIGURE 9.10 Since this artwork is symmetrical, I only have to build half of the content. Once that's done, I just copy and flip it. (Review "Symmetry Is Your Friend" in chapter 6.)

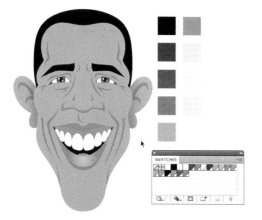

FIGURE 9.11 Once I have all of my core base vector shapes finished, I then start to work out the colors I'll be using in my design. I might think about color earlier than this, but I avoid any actual color work until I have the form of all of my shapes established. I also start to organize my file using layers.

FIGURE 9.12 At this point, I move away from the computer and go back into the analog realm, drawing out the shading shapes exactly how I'll build them on a printout of the art. (For more information about this back-and-forth process, review chapter 3.)

FIGURE 9.13 With my shading drawn out, I scan it in and move back to Illustrator, building the new vector shapes based on the new shaded sketch.

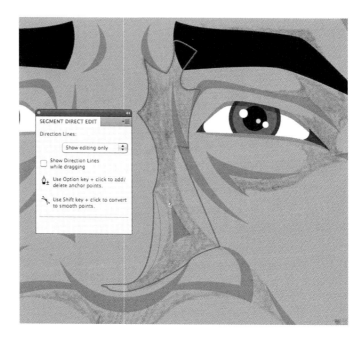

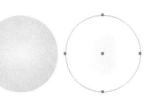

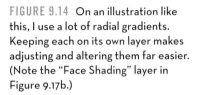

FIGURE 9.14 On an illustration like this, I use a lot of radial gradients. Keeping each on its own layer makes adjusting and altering them far easier. (Note the "Face Shading" layer in Figure 9.17b.)

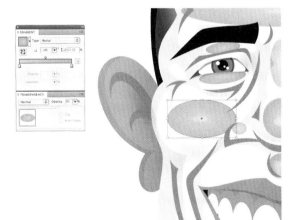

FIGURE 9.15 Keeping each radial gradients on its own layer also makes fine-tuning the blend modes easier. I can arrange each layer in the layering hierarchy so that it works well with my design. In this illustration, I keep them below the vector shapes for the face shading. (To fully appreciate the flexibility afforded by layering, deconstruct the resource file called "Obama," which you'll find on the DVD.)

FIGURE 9.16 Using layers helps me keep track of all the detailed elements in an illustration. Being able to isolate content and turn layers on and off at will helps focus my attention on detail and allows me to achieve the visual effects I want.

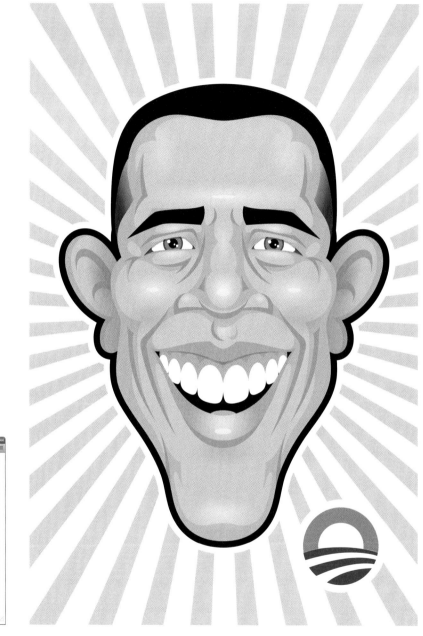

FIGURE 9.17A Final caricature design titled "Head of State." Creating and editing this design was far more efficient using layers than it would have been trying to do everything on one single layer.

FIGURE 9.17B Note how I have logically ordered the content of this illustration and labeled each layer to clearly define what it contains (see box above left). If, say, I have to open this file up four years from now, I won't have to guess how I layered my vectors. Using an organized layering system is a good creative habit that you'll appreciate more and more every year.

How to Avoid the Basement

All drawing programs have layers. Within Adobe Illustrator, there are two types of layers. To help you understand both types, think of your drawing as a house that has a ground floor—your living area—and a scary basement. The ground floor is like the top-level layer in Illustrator. The basement is equivalent to the sub-layer in Illustrator (FIGURE 9.18).

Illustrator automatically creates sub-layers; you can't avoid it. Every layer has a sub-layer; fortunately, you should never have to go there.

1. **Top-Level Layer:** If you layer your vector designs using common sense, as described earlier, you'll rarely, if ever, have to go into the sub-layers. I should also point out that naming your top levels appropriately will help you find your way around in your design, too.

2. **Sub-Layers:** Whatever top-level layer you are building on, Illustrator will automatically create the sub-layers for it. You should rarely have to drill down into that basement. But it's important to be aware that sub-layers exist, regardless if you ever decide to use them.

FIGURE 9.18 Think of your top-level layers as your living space. The sub-layer is the scary basement. Consider the Obama illustration again. The top level layering is shown on the left, and the sub-layers that each of the top-level layers contain are waterfalled out on the right—scary! But as long as you have your top-level layering organized, there really is no reason to dive any deeper into the sub-layers.

Combining Build Method with Layering

In chapter 6 we discussed how dissecting your vector shapes into smaller, more manageable pieces can assist you in constructing a larger whole. That same principle can be applied to the composition of your entire design.

Some projects just work best if you handle them in a modular fashion. In this next example, I broke one project into two pieces—a foreground and a background—so I could better focus on the specifics of each. Later, I combined them to form one composition (**FIGURES 9.19–9.29**).

In this project, I really had to depend on smart layering to manage all of the detail and make controlling my vector graphics easier (**FIGURES 9.19–9.29**).

FIGURE 9.19 A thumbnail sketch for a Japanese-inspired repeat pattern design that will form the background for the final project.

FIGURE 9.20 My refined sketch for the repeat pattern design. Since the blossom shapes are so geometric, I don't need to waste time drawing them out precisely. I can easily create them using the Ellipse tool (L).

FIGURE 9.21 All of the vines and leaves were created utilizing TCM and PPP via the point-to-point method that we covered in chapters 5 and 6. The rest of the content was created using the shape-building method covered in chapter 6. I now have all of my base vector shapes that will form the final pattern design.

FIGURES 9.22–9.23
Using layers, I create a three-level hierarchy. Each is set to various transparencies to achieve the visual aesthetic that I'm after. My repeat pattern design for the background is now complete (shown at right) so I begin the second piece of the project, the foreground.

FIGURE 9.24 This was the first time I had to illustrate in this style. I spent about a day refining my sketch so that I could build my vector shapes on top of it as precisely as possible.

FIGURE 9.25 I needed to use the point-by-point build method for most of this drawing to achieve this specific look. The only shape-building method I used was in the pupils of the eyes since they are circular in shape. Every other vector shape was discerned using TCM and PPP. Notice how I dissected my vector shapes into smaller, more manageable pieces. (You can review all of these methods in chapters 5 and 6.)

FIGURE 9.26 As I created this artwork, I logically organized its content using top-level layers only, as shown at left. Illustrator, of course, automatically created the numerous sub-layers shown at right. But I never had to touch them to create this artwork.

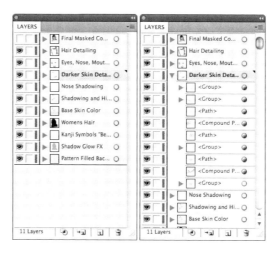

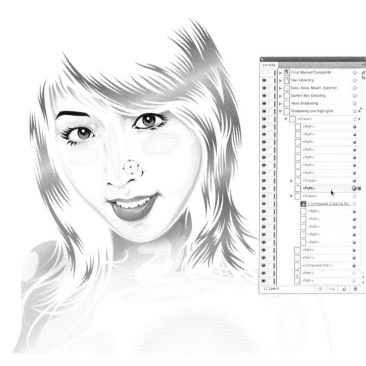

FIGURE 9.27 If you organize your top-level layers well, you'll never need to drill down into the sub-layers. To do so, however, you simply click the gray triangle on the top-level layer and the sub-layers will flow below it (indented). The sub-layers on a complex illustration like this could number in the hundreds and even contain additional secondary sub-layers within them. If you choose to go into the basement of your art, it can get pretty cluttered, as shown in the box at left.

FIGURE 9.28 If you take the time to arrange your top-level layers coherently, naming them in such a way that you know what you're dealing with, then you can avoid navigating the needless layer bloat that is sub-layers.

FIGURE 9.29 I combine the repeat pattern design and my illustration into one unified composition to form my final illustration called "Beautiful." The good creative habit of layering made the creative process a lot easier and faster.

Colors and File Naming

I debated whether to include this material in the book because it's more related to personal preference than anything else, and it's a little anal retentive, too. But I still think it's important to at least touch on it briefly since we deal with colors and file naming every day.

When you work digitally the more you can automate routine functions and set preferences, the more efficient and easier your work will be.

When it comes to color swatches in Adobe Illustrator, it's smart to create a custom set of colors that you use on a regular basis so you don't have to re-create the wheel each time you work on a new project.

It's simple: Just add your preferred colors to your Swatches palette, double-click the swatch, and make sure to check the Global check box (**FIGURE 9.30**). This makes using your selected colors, as well as performing universal or global edits of your preferred palette, quick and easy. If you don't click the Global box, you'll have to manually select every vector shape that uses the color you want to change, one at a time, and then make the change.

I also like to visually arrange my color swatches so that they run from light to dark. This makes selecting the right color faster than it otherwise would be if I had to scan and rescan a random assortment of colors when building my designs.

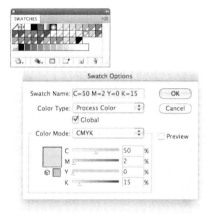

FIGURE 9.30 Every artist has his or her own specific palettes. My projects often need flesh tones, so I've included those. Whatever colors you find yourself using over and over again are good candidates for your color presets.

Once you've created your custom set of color swatches, you can add it to your start-up profile so that every new document you open will contain that palette (also review "Create a New Document Profile" in chapter 2).

A Typical Project Folder

Digital creatives work with electronic files every day. On my workstation alone, I have 973,493 individual files, and these files are found in 263,341 folders. It goes without saying that having a file naming standard to keep track of your work will make finding specific files a whole lot easier.

I wish someone would have clued me in on this back in the mid-1990s when I first got started. It would have saved me a lot of time over the years, fruitlessly looking for long-forgotten file names and never finding the vector art I knew I had somewhere in my archive.

As shown in **FIGURE 9.31**, my file naming is methodical, and I keep it simple to aid in my future searches. As shown in **FIGURE 9.32**, a typical Glitschka Studios project folder contains:

Project_Name_Build.ai   Project_Name_Comp_v1.ai

Project_Name_Final.ai   Project_Name_Whatever.ai

FIGURE 9.31 This image shows how I name my files. Project_Name_Build.ai contains all of my build elements for every direction provided. If I needed to harvest an element later, I'd access this file. Project_Name_Comp.ai is what I present to the client for approval. Project_Name_Final.ai is the final art. I use this same hierarchical standard for every variation of a project that has its own file.

- **Build File:** The staging and building area for the vector creative work

- **Refined Sketches:** Used to place inside my drawing program

- **Project Specs:** Compiled notes for quick referencing

- **Email:** Key correspondence between the client and me

- **Old Files:** Secondary documents, reference material, research, unicorns, and so on

- **Files Sent:** Presentation, comps, and final art files

Creating color swatches and maintaining file naming standards aren't what I'd consider creative work, but they are good creative habits that will facilitate your workflow and allow you more time to focus on what you'd rather be doing. In that respect, it's worth the initial investment to get your creative house in order.

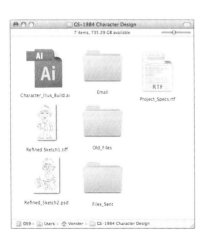

FIGURE 9.32 This image shows a typical project file here at Glitschka Studios. The project number in the folder name corresponds with the invoicing system I have established with my CPA to track job invoices sent out.

Last, But Not Least

Nothing will benefit you more as a creative person than to establish, practice, and relentlessly refine your creative process as a design professional. The benefits from doing so will be self-evident. The systematic creative processes I document in this book can greatly assist you in this regard.

But generalities aside, I'm speaking to you now, mano a mano. You know yourself. You know all of the bad creative proclivities you gravitate toward. So I ask you, from this moment forward, to resist the urge to be a tooler (review chapter 3), and pursue your creative career with design excellence at the forefront of your mind. Be purposeful in your dedication to creating quality art and producing your ideas with precision in vector form.

Set aside those bad creative habits that hold you back, and implement the methods and insights I've shared. Review your processes often to hold yourself creatively accountable. Add good habits to your workflow, adapt them, and improve them so you can go forth and create and grow at levels you have never known before.

Here endeth the lesson.

> "Failure is not fatal, but failure to change might be."
> — JOHN WOODEN

FIELD NOTES

VBT Wants You!

The learning process should never end. We should all continually strive to grow in our creative pursuits, and there's no better way of doing this than to share knowledge with one another.

After you've read through this book and watched all of the tutorials on the included DVD, I encourage you to enroll in the *Vector Basic Training* Facebook group. There, you'll be able to share your own methods, insights, and creative good habits with others in the design community so we can all benefit.

Enroll in the VBT Facebook page here: http://goo.gl/esQ9D.

DESIGN DRILLS:
Top-Eight List

One of the hardest questions I'm asked as a creative is, "What is your favorite piece of artwork?" I usually answer the same way every time: "The piece I'm working on right now."

I tend to grow tired of my own work pretty quickly, truth be told.

That said, I particularly like the following pieces—either because of what they say to me personally or because of the experiences I associate with them.

I hope *you* enjoy all of the artwork used in this book, but more importantly, I hope that you benefit from the methods I've shared with you so that you can enjoy creating your own work even more.

FIGURE 9.33 This owl will always hold a fond place in my heart because it was the first illustration of mine to be accepted into the New York Society of Illustrators. Knowing my work hung on the same walls as Norman Rockwell's work is just too stinking cool.

FIGURE 9.34 I don't normally engage in political artwork, but it was very cathartic
to take an assortment of cultural woes, conspiracies, and pop-culture items that
captivated my own thinking at the time and wrap them into a compelling poster
design called "Last Daze," which was part of a national traveling art show called
Propaganda III.

FIGURE 9.35 Sometimes I create a piece of art and when I'm done I have no idea why. That kind of happened here. When I was done, the title "Temporal Infestation" came to mind, and that made perfect sense to me.

FIGURE 9.36 The continuous-line style is a challenging but fun approach to illustration. This collection of linear "Squiggle Heads" was created for an art book project out of the UK called *Human*. I just like the personality I was able to capture in each figure via one single line.

FIGURE 9.37 When you do work for ad agencies, you never know if they'll end up using what you've created. Many times I'll create something I love, but it will never see the light of day. Such was the case for this concept illustration for a line of Indian tea. Even though this design was never used, I still love the composition, balance, and color.

FIGURE 9.38 When it comes to tattoos, I'm a weenie: I don't have any. I don't like pain, but mainly it's because I can't commit to my art for a lifetime. That said, I love this tribal tattoo style. It's a good mix of design and hard-core flair that's fun to work with. This design is called "Talon."

FIGURE 9.38 I've always like my "Suicide King" illustration. It's a fun, quirky, and colorful take on the classic motif utilizing one of my favorite styles. It was used in a group art project for a custom card deck.

FIGURE 9.39 He's simple, iconic, yet powerful—not to mention loaded with nearly ever pirate visual pun you can use, sans a parrot on the shoulder. Arrrrgh! I created this avatar icon for a collectible game for kids produced by Upper Deck.

Index

A

Actions, 27–29
Add Anchor Point tool, 18
Adobe Illustrator. *See also individual tools*
  color swatches in, 219
  core tools for vector building in, 17–22
  customizing, 26–28
  layers in, 213
  shortcomings of, 16–17, 32–33, 134
  toggling modes in, 11
Alignment Guides, 27
anchor points
  adding, 18
  bad, 74
  converting, 19, 77, 122
  corner, 72–73, 100, 101
  deleting, 18
  good, 72–73, 80–81, 83–86
  importance of, 71–72, 100
  incorrect, 75, 77, 82, 104
  placing, 87–109
  preferences for, 26
  Prime Point Placement of, 72, 89, 100–103,
    104, 109
  rounding off, 24–25
  selecting, 19

  smooth, 73, 100, 101, 122
  spotting potential problems with, 76–79
  wrong number of, 105–7, 125
art direction
  fresh eyes effect, 182–84
  importance of, 181–82, 194
  vector building and, 185–89
  visual tension and, 189–94

B

"Beautiful," 218
"Beloved Virus" clothing, 57–61
Bernstein, Sergei Natanovich, 3
BetterHandles plug-in, 17, 134–35
Bézier, Paul, 4–5, 7
Bézier curves
  benefits of, 9
  determining need for, 8
  equation of, 6
  examples of, 11–14
  flat, 78
  history of, 3–4
Big Bocca, 170–73
"Blinky," 111
"Body & Soul," 11–12
Bring to Front Again shortcut, 29

C

Casselman, Bill, 6
Citroën, 3, 4
The Clockwork Method (TCM)
 basics of, 88–90
 combining Prime Point Placement and, 102–3
 for complex shapes, 97–99
 examples of, 89, 90–99, 108–9, 113–16, 165
Clone shortcut, 28
colors, 219
complacency, 194
Convert Anchor Point tool, 19
CorelDraw, 16
creative habits
 colors, 219
 doodling, 202, 203–5, 206
 file naming, 219–20
 importance of good, 201–3
 layering, 205–18
 setting aside bad, 221
creative process
 analog tools for, 45
 foundation for, 44
 healthy, 145
 refinement and, 49–56, 221
 systematic, 57–61
 thumbnailing and, 45–49

D

"Day of the Dead," 35–37
de Casteljau, Paul, 3, 4
de Casteljau algorithm, 3
Delete Anchor Point tool, 18
Deselect shortcut, 29
"Digital Lifestyle," 202
Direct Selection tool, 19, 122
doodling, 45, 63–66, 202, 203–5, 206. *See also* thumbnailing

drawing
 analog tools for, 45
 determining end of, 62
 importance of, 42–44
 improving, 61–62
 refining, 49–56
 thumbnails, 45–49
"DZGN-BOT," 161

E

Ellipse tool, 20, 126, 127, 130, 133, 142, 159, 209, 214
"Escape," 67
Exclude shape mode, 20, 21

F

Facebook, 221
Fanta Phantom character, 132
Feed Your Imagination, 161
file naming, 219–20
Flora, Jim, 158
Freehand, 11, 15, 23
fresh eyes effect, 182–84

G

graphic style, 31–32, 170–73

H

handles
 example of, 8
 isolating, 19
 manipulating, 19
 overextended, 78, 79, 105
 parallel, 78, 79
 preferences for, 26
 revealing, 19
"Head of State," 212
Human, 226

I

ideas
    capturing, in thumbnails, 45–49
    generating, 44
    refining, 49–56
Inkscape, 16
Intersect shape mode, 20, 21, 177

K

Keyboard Characters, 158–62
keyboard shortcuts, 27–29

L

"Last Daze," 224
layers
    efficiency of, 205–12
    establishing structure of, 32–40
    top-level vs. sub-, 213
linear line style, 154–57
logos, 52–53, 57–61, 115, 136–38, 170–73, 192–93
"Loyal Order of Wormwood," 38–40

M

Major League Baseball (MLB) licensed products, 83–84
Make Clipping Mask shortcut, 28
math, attitude toward, 2–3
"Mickey Rat," 175–80
Minus Front shape mode, 20, 21, 127, 128, 130, 133, 139, 142

N

National Basketball Association (NBA) licensed products, 83–84
new document profile, creating, 29–31
New York Society of Illustrators, 223
Nineblock Software, 134–35
"Nisqually," 13–14

O

Obama, Barack, 208–12
Outline mode, 11

P

Pathfinder panel, 20–21, 126, 127, 130, 133, 134, 176–78. *See also individual functions*
Pen tool, 17, 18
Pepsi, 115
perspective, changing, 82
"Pet Monster," 161
point-by-point method
    examples of, 110, 119
    steps in, 122–25
    using, 118, 129
Preferences, 26–27
Preview mode, 11
Prime Point Placement (PPP), 72, 89, 100–103, 104, 109
Propaganda III, 224

R

Rectangle tool, 20, 126
Reflect tool, 22, 139, 143, 147, 171, 197
Release Clipping Mask shortcut, 28
Remove Redundant Points, 134
"Riled Rover," 158–62
risk taking, 194
Rock and Roll Hall of Fame, 163–69
Rotate tool, 22, 133
Round Fillet tool, 22

S

St. Martin's Press, 148, 152
Scale Strokes & Effects, 26
Segment Direct Edit tool, 22, 23, 121
segmented style, 158–62
Selection tool, 19
Send to Back shortcut, 29

shape-building method
  examples of, 59, 119
  steps in, 126–28
  throw-away shapes in, 132–33
  using, 118, 129
shapes
  dissecting design into smaller, 136–37, 147–50
  practicing discerning, 112
  visual tension and, 189–94
signature styles, 151, 158
Smart Guides, 27, 32, 33
Smart Remove tool, 135
Smart Rounding filter, 22
Snapping Tolerance, 27
"Squiggle Heads," 226
startup profile, 30–31
style boards, 174
styles
  choosing, 152
  exploring new, 152, 174
  graphic, 31–32, 170–73
  linear line, 154–57
  segmented, 158–62
  signature, 151, 158
  tribal tattoo, 163–69
"Suicide King," 229
Symmetric Edit tool, 22
symmetry, benefiting from, 139–43, 147–50

T
"Talon," 228
TCM. See The Clockwork Method
"Temporal Infestation," 225
"Thug Bunny," 195–200
thumbnailing, 45–49, 68–69. See also doodling
"Tickles, the Evil Clown," 144
tribal tattoo style, 163–69
Tri3ye, 54–56
"Twitter Beard," 70

U
Ungroup shortcut, 29
Unite shape mode, 20, 21, 128, 139, 142, 143, 178, 196
Unite shortcut, 29
Upper Deck, 230

V
vector building
  core tools for, 17–25
  layering and, 214–18
  methods for, 117–33
  self-art direction and, 185–89
  symmetry and, 139–43
vector skeletons, 83–86
Veer, 86
visual tension, 189–94, 198

W
Warp tool, 22
Wayne Enterprises, 152
Weierstrass, Karl, 3
Weierstrass theorem, 3

X
Xtream Path plug-in, 17, 22, 23–25, 121, 178, 196, 209

Z
ZuPreem, 116

Designated Doodle Area

WATCH
READ
CREATE

Meet Creative Edge.

A new resource of unlimited books, videos and tutorials for creatives from the world's leading experts.

Creative Edge is your one stop for inspiration, answers to technical questions and ways to stay at the top of your game so you can focus on what you do best—being creative.

All for only $24.99 per month for access—any day any time you need it.

creative
edge

peachpit.com/creativeedge

Designated Doodle Area